FINDING THE TREASURE WITHIN YOU

by

JIM LEWIS

DeVorss and Company
P.O. Box 550
Marina del Rey, California 90291

Copyright © 1982
by Jim Lewis

4/93

ISBN: 0-87516-469-2
Library of Congress Card Catalog Number: 81-70339

Printed in the United States of America by
Book Graphics, Inc., California

Other Books by the Author:

Positive Thoughts for Successful Living

Mystical Teachings of Christianity

Reincarnation & Translation (booklet)

How to Think Like a Winner

The Great Commitment

I would like to dedicate this book to Kathy Robinson, my secretary, who is an invaluable help to me in the preparation of all my books.

PREFACE

There is more than a gold mine within you. The treasure within you is worth more than all the money or gold in the world. No one can steal your treasure and it will never be lost or used up—it is infinite and unlimited.

You may know already that this treasure is there and you may be wondering how you can tap this rich Source. The ideas in this book will help you. They have helped me and many others.

This treasure cannot be measured in terms of money, for you will find many blessings come into your life without money. Money cannot buy happiness, peace of mind, inner security and outer harmony. Money cannot buy love and companionship. When money is needed, it will be provided you can be sure.

Jesus said, "Seek ye first the kingdom of God and all these things will be added." The "things" were the outer, material things such as food, clothing, money, and whatever was necessary to make our lives comfortable and successful. The road or path to the kingdom may seem to be challenging to walk, but any other way is even more so, for any other way will only lead to defeat no matter how promising it seems to be.

The words of Jesus, "Seek and ye shall find," encourage us to search diligently for that treasure within, and I trust you will find it.

Jim Lewis

Denver, Colorado
1981

CONTENTS

"TREASURES IN HEAVEN"

A rich man came to Jesus one day and asked how he might gain eternal life. When Jesus told him to sell all he had and give it to the poor, he left very sad. The man was attached to his riches and Jesus was trying to help him realize that he needed instead to have that dependence on God in consciousness. Jesus then said it would be difficult for a rich man to enter the kingdom. This was not because God would make it so, but because of this tendency to put our faith and trust in things. Some poor people have this problem as well.

Jesus then said on another occasion, "Lay not up for yourselves treasures upon the earth, where moth and rust doth consume, and where thieves break through and steal; but lay up for yourselves treasures in heaven, where neither moth nor rust doth consume, and where thieves do not break through nor steal: for where thy treasure is, there will thy heart be also." (Mat. 6:19–22)

We spend much of our time, effort, money, thought, and energy seeking to store up earthly treasures, "things." We become attached to these treasures and feel they are essential to our happiness and well-being. Sometimes having many things, especially money, gives us a false or inadequate or incomplete sense of security in them. If they are destroyed or stolen we are upset. Some people have actually committed suicide over their losses.

What are the treasures in heaven and how do we store them up? Jesus is talking about consciousness. Only what is yours in consciousness is permanent. If you have consciousness you will always have things provided. Even if

1

things are destroyed they will be restored. If they are stolen they will be replaced. When consciousness is developed, God can do His good works through us. In Psalm 127:1 we are told, "Unless the Lord builds the house, those who build it labor in vain." Those who work on the personal, human level seeking to build happiness and security don't think they are laboring in vain. They listen to the prophets of false promises saying, "Get in there and pitch and you'll become rich." It is rather sad to see all this useless labor they put forth, often with much enthusiasm and expectation, and yet not gain what they are seeking. However, they must realize that it is useless labor before they can give the "Lord" within them an opportunity to build a true consciousness that will manifest all that they need, a consciousness of God that will guide them and give them spiritual understanding.

There is an easier way to build this inner consciousness. It may seem to be more difficult but it really isn't. I am going to tell you about this way from a few personal experiences. I didn't discover or invent it but I began realizing it in 1953. There were some good books and teachers along the way that helped but the inner work had to be done by me, or at least I had to be ready and willing to let God do the inner work.

The first thing I realized through my seeking and study and prayer was that we become aware of that to which we give our time, thought, interest and energy. If we want the treasures in heaven then that is what we must seek. Treasures in heaven will produce all kinds of earthly treasures, but earthly treasures will not produce treasures in heaven. Another thing I had to realize is that if we seek the treasures in heaven for the earthly results, we'll not find either. Prayer is the fastest, easiest, and most profitable way to develop the treasures in heaven. Many times we are willing to do all kinds of things. I learned early that the more I prayed the better I felt and the better things worked out.

When I began in 1953 I was loaded with problems. I was in my mid-twenties and single, and that was a big problem in my thinking. I didn't like my work and I didn't know what I really wanted to do. I thought I only wanted to get rich so I wouldn't have to work.

Unity helped me change all that. When I read the book, *Lessons in Truth*, I knew that I had to find out more about the God within me. All I knew about was a God that was supposed to be up in the skies. I felt like one of His rejects. I began in earnest to read voraciously and to begin praying. I really didn't know how to pray but in my talking with God I began to learn.

I began attending classes and services at the local Unity Church. During the week I followed this type of a schedule: each day before I went to work I would sit down and read some inspirational literature and then spend some time in prayer. During my lunch hour I would sometimes come home, get a quick lunch and then pray. Sometimes I would stay at work and go out in the parking lot to my car and spend the hour there in a time of prayer. In the evenings I would sometimes go to a spot out on an island and sit there for several hours in a time of contemplative prayer, sometimes with my eyes closed and sometimes with them open. I couldn't talk about these new ideas with my mother so I learned to talk with God. I spent my time talking and learning to listen to how He talked to me.

It finally dawned on me that He was talking to me. I thought in the beginning that the way to tell how he communicated His guidance to us was that it would always be something I wanted to do. Was I ever wrong! I was so busy trying to talk Him into making me what I wanted to be. I asked Him to make me a really successful salesman. I promised I would give Him a fair share of the money and I promised I wouldn't let it go to my head, that I would keep going to church on Sundays and a few other things. He said, "I have other plans for you." When I found out what those plans were, I was disappointed. The last thing I would ever have put on any human treasure map at that time was to be a minister. But I kept on praying. Peace finally came when I accepted what He was guiding me to do. Realizing what was before me would have overwhelmed me if I had not made the commitment to trust Him for everything. I had never read the Bible, knew nothing about church history or much of any other history. The only Jesus I knew about was the sad one I was told about in church. When I learned to read the scriptures I found out He was totally different from that other "Church" Jesus.

When I arrived at Unity Village to study for the ministry I kept up my prayer times. When I had time off I prayed. Each day before work I would go up early to work and sit in the prayer room for a half hour before the other workers came in, spending that time in prayer.

The big challenge came when I was seeking guidance as to where I would go when I finished school. I was still very human and asked God to make it a nice church with adequate funds and no problems, and especially for it to be in Florida, where I grew up. That wasn't to be; it was in Washington, D.C. When they asked me to go to Washington for two weeks to look into this church as a possibility I knew inside that God was behind it. I went, though, hoping that it wouldn't happen. I wanted the minister there to say no. Instead he welcomed me. I spent most of that two weeks praying, for I knew this would be a challenge. There was no church building, no church funds, and not much of a congregation—just 20 people meeting on Sunday in a small hotel room. Total assets were about 50 hymn books and an old lectern. I had plenty of time to pray while I was there, practically day and night. I rented a car one day trying to find a place to stay when I would get there and found nothing. However, I figured that God was behind all this and that one would be provided.

My wife and I and our two-year-old daughter arrived in

Washington, D.C. on Easter Sunday in 1959 in our car and U-haul trailer. We didn't have much in the way of furniture and therefore needed a furnished house to live in. I had been told it would be practically impossible to find one, especially one that didn't require a lease. However, the first one we decided to call from the ads in the paper was a beautiful home, completely furnished, on an acre of wooded land. And to top it off, the owner didn't want a lease.

There were times during the next five months when I really didn't know how we would survive, but God always came through. Attendance and income picked up. I was able to rent a small office across the street from the hotel as well as larger quarters in the hotel for the Sunday meeting. I still had plenty of time and I spent that time praying. Before the office was opened, about a month, I had nothing to do during the week but pray. I spent so much time praying that my wife thought I might be doing a little sleeping, but I wasn't.

Though it was a challenging experience I shall always value this time. I discovered more about God and realized that He can provide even in the most severe circumstances if I only remain in that consciousness of trust and let Him open the doors. I can't begin to tell of the many marvelous ways He worked to guide us and take care of us.

Prayer isn't something we do until we get some results; it is something we do forever if we are serious about our spiritual growth. Prayer, or meditation if you like that word, builds the treasure in heaven, the consciousness of trust in God. When we have that treasure in heaven, whether it is a small treasure, small awareness, or a grand one, the consciousness of God will always take care of us no matter what the outer circumstances of our lives may be. With that kind of inner assurance we can go forward in peace and confidence and discover a wonderful new life.

ACCEPTING THE CHALLENGE

A few years ago I became interested in scuba diving. I thought it would be an interesting way to take a vacation and see what was going on below the surface of the ocean or some lake or spring. I knew it would be challenging, for although I liked the water, the thought of going down 50 or 100 feet below the surface raised some apprehensive thoughts and feelings. It would have been easy for me to have talked myself out of it. All the reasons against it came to mind with powerful, persuading influence. I had to deal with the "what ifs," the suppositions that usually frighten us but hardly ever happen. What if I ran out of air way down there? What if I ran into sharks, barracudas, or some other so-called vicious fish? I had experienced the pain of pressure just from going down in swimming pools; what would this be like going down much further? In spite of these and other questions, I accepted the challenge and enrolled in the course.

I had to accept the possibility that everything suggested by my fearful thinking would happen. I didn't know whether these things would or would not happen. Fortunately none of them did. In the course we were told how to deal with these possibilities and be prepared. I found that if a person did what he or she was told to do there were no problems. I am glad now that I accepted the challenge. I would have missed seeing and enjoying a beautiful world. Seeing pictures of this world is not the same. Just think of what I would have missed if I had let my fears and apprehensions be my guide. There is a great deal of truth in Emerson's statement, "Do the thing you fear and the death of fear is certain."

For everything we want to do in life to bring about improvement or increase our knowledge or ability there is a challenge connected with it. If you want more education, it will be challenging to get it. The challenge will include more than just asking and answering positively whether you have the ability or not. If you want healing, it will be challenging to get it. If you want harmony and peace there will be challenges involved in bringing them about. If you want spiritual growth, it will be challenging to do what is necessary to gain that supreme gift, the knowledge of the Presence of God. By knowledge I mean more than intellectual knowledge, I mean spiritual awareness.

The challenge is as great or even greater for the individual involved in some negative pursuit. The thief planning to steal will have his challenges. The one who attempts repeatedly to avoid or get out of doing what he or she knows should be done will also have challenges.

When we are able to sort out our many desires we find that many of them are spiritually right. The desire for control and mastery of our lives, the desire for health, the desire for guidance, and the great number one desire, the desire to know God, are all legitimate desires. We don't always want to accept what is necessary for the fulfillment of these desires. Negative reasons will always try to persuade us to reject the challenges associated with the good. This reasoning may be in the form of such questions as, "Is it worth it?" or "Will it really work?"

If we are to achieve the good that God has in store for us we must accept the challenges associated with the receiving of that good. If we are to have God's prosperity and success we must be willing to learn the principles of supply and use them as God guides us. Many want the result without making the effort. They seek ways around the principle. For example, in regards to supply, giving is much more important than using the imagination in visualizing. Yet many would rather visualize than give.

Many often spend more time, energy, and money trying

to avoid the challenges than in meeting them, but this is a futile attempt. The greater our expectations the greater the challenges seem to us in human consciousnes. But remember, that is only the way they seem. We should remember that with God all challenges can be met successfully.

One of our first big steps is getting to the point where we are willing to accept the right solution to the challenge. The right way may seem to be the worst way, the hardest way, and the longest way. But really it is the best, the easiest, and the shortest way. Some have to discover this after many misadventures over long periods of time. Some people deal with challenges by cutting off all positive expectation. For the moment it may seem psychologically best, for it removes the pressures usually associated with challenges and the acceptance of challenges. But one day we must accept the challenge and grow. Delay doesn't make anything easier.

Probably our biggest challenge in life will be the challenge of accepting spiritual growth. We know that to know God will solve all problems. It seems that to seek Him will cost us too much. It seems we will lose more than we will gain but that is always a false assumption.

Paul, the Apostle, is a good case for study and learning from someone's experience. He was a Jew, born in Tarsus to a well-to-do family. He was about Jesus' age. He lived his early years in a Greek environment but when he was about sixteen or seventeen his parents sent him to Jerusalem to study with some well-known and respected rabbis. He became very zealous in his religious pursuit, the study of the law and obedience to the law. He thought that absolute adherence to the laws of Moses would please God. He said of himself that he was a "Hebrew of Hebrews." He was dedicated. He had an intense zeal to conform to the law. He had a bold confidence and dogged persistence. He had a blind but absolute trust and belief that he was doing what was right.

When this developing new sect of Jewish Christians got out of hand he thought it was his duty to try and stop it. He pursued this end with all his strength and ability and determination. When a person has all this commitment going, something has to happen, and it did with Paul on the road to Damascus. He could have charged the experience up to one big hallucination and decided he needed some rest before he continued his hot pursuit of the Christians. He could have stayed right where he was spiritually. But he didn't; he accepted the challenge. He didn't know where it would lead. He didn't say, "Tell me what you want me to do before I decide I will do it." He didn't know how long it would take—he discovered it was a lifetime. He didn't know whether he would be healed—he was now physically blind.

Paul always wanted to do the right thing; his problem was that he didn't know what the right thing was. He had been trained in a tradition that wasn't wholly true. But now he knew what was right and he was willing to accept the challenge of growing and doing what God guided him to do. Although it meant giving up a great deal, he was willing to do it. Without this willingness to do whatever the Spirit guided him to do he would not have been able to accept this great challenge in his spiritual growth. He wasn't looking just to achieve success, but he was a greater success than he ever thought he would be. For him success was a by-product. He found greater happiness than he would ever have found in the way he was going. It was always a struggle to listen to and follow the Presence that was seeking to use him. The struggle wasn't because of God but because of his past conditioning. If it had not been for such a strict conditioning, things might have been quite different and less difficult. But his achievements were great because he accepted the challenge on that Damascus road.

God within you can guide you through any challenge in

your life. If you are willing to accept whatever He guides you to do you will find yourself experiencing greater good—healing, supply, happiness, and much more. If you will spend more time seeking Him, listening for His voice in your times of meditation, you will get answers that will enable you to meet all challenges of growth successfully. But you will have to be dedicated as was Paul. You will have to persevere and be patient. You will have to stand firm even when your own thoughts are filled with discouragement. You will have to keep your expectations high. This is more than a human desire, for this is a knowing that certain things are right and an assumption that they will be made manifest.

With God there is no failure, only success and the joy of knowing that success is in God.

"I AM THE WAY . . ."

Jesus made some statements that seem, from the human viewpoint, very puzzling and difficult to comprehend. These statements begin with the words, "I AM." Before we can understand these statements we must consider some personal remarks he made.

For example, in John 14:24, Jesus said, "The word which you hear is not mine but the Father's who sent me." Even though the words came through Jesus and he was heard speaking them, nevertheless He said they were not His personal remarks. In John 14:10, it is recorded that Jesus said, "Do you not believe that I am in the Father and the Father in me? The words that I say to you I do not speak on my own authority, but the Father who dwells in me does his works." In other words, Jesus is saying that there are times when He is speaking above the personal level and that the Father is speaking through Him.

When the words, "Come unto me . . ." came through Jesus they were not meant personally. Jesus is not here physically so it would be impossible to come to Him. Joining the church is not coming to Jesus. It was not to the personal individual Jesus that we were to come but to God within us.

The "I AM" statement that we are concerned with here is the one that reads, "I am the way, and the truth, and the life; no one comes to the Father, but by Me." (John 14:6) The "I AM" and the "Me" are identical, and it is through the I AM that we reach the Father. But what are the I AM and the Father?

11

I AM was an Old Testament designation for God. Moses was told by God that he should tell the people that "I AM hath sent me unto you." He was also told, "This shall be my name forevermore." I AM is God's name in you, in me, and in Jesus. It is the universal nature of God individualized and made personal. It is the name that we are not to take in vain as stated in the third commandment, "You shall not take the name of the Lord your God in vain." The usual interpretation of this commandment is that we should not cuss or swear using God's name. That is a very immature perception of the meaning of this great commandment. What it really means is that we should not use the power of God within us in a negative and limiting way. We should not identify the great power of the I AM with anything negative, such as saying, "I am sick, poor, etc."

The word "Father" is used to identify the universal nature of God—God omnipresent. The laws of God are universal. When we have a consciousness or awareness of the indwelling God, the I AM, we are then in the consciousness of the omnipresence. In this consciousness there is no time nor space to be overcome. There is not past or present, only the eternal now. Yes, we may remember things that happened in the past but they are nothing, for the past is no more, there is only the present and that is all there will ever be. No one can live in the past or in the future, only in the present. One may think about the past and the future but that is quite different from living in them. We can only live now, right now in the present.

When Jesus said, "I am the way . . ." He was telling us that the only access we have to the Father, universal God-consciousness, is through the indwelling I AM, God individualized in us. When Jesus said, "I and my Father are one" it was His way of stating that the universal and the individual are always one. There is no separation between ourselves and God; we are one as Jesus was one. The only difference is that Jesus knew his oneness with God. His knowing was a full conscious realization. We at most have only a small awareness of this great truth. We may have much intellectual knowledge about it and may be able to express this knowledge very fluently. So, the way to God is within you, through the I AM.

Referring to the way to God, Jesus said, "Narrow is the gate and strait is the way, which leads to life, and few there be that find it." (Mat. 7:14) The way to God-consciousness or God-awareness is strait and undeviating; there are no exceptions or dispensations. We may take a circuitous route trying to get there but that is only because as human beings we have a great tendency of looking for the quick, easy way to everything and often wind up taking the long, hard way instead.

Jesus also said there was another way that humans often follow. He said it had a wide gate and broad way but that it leads to destruction. He said many would go in that gate and walk in that way. That way is the human way, the way of seeking our happiness and good in sensory living. This way seems to offer us so much. We are told by well-meaning but misinformed individuals that it is quick and easy and that if we only put forth some personal effort we can eat the great plums of life. The majority will never eat the plums of material living. Sure, more millionaires are made every year but when we consider the total increase in population the increase is paltry. There will be many who seek the plums, for they will listen to the call and the cry of those who make simplistic promises. But the plums will always seem to be "just around the corner." Even the plums that are plucked will not have a lasting effect. No millionaire is ever satisfied and says "this is enough."

This may seem pessimistic, but it is telling it like it is. There is only one way to lasting happiness and satisfaction and that is through God, the I AM within you. When you do what God tells you to do, then and only then will you

be satisfied. It can't be any other way. You will be satisfied whether you have money or don't have it. If you have
God-consciousness and need money, it will be provided. If
you have God-consciousness and need anything, it will be
provided. When we do what God guides us to do we find
true happiness and we are truly "filled" to overflowing
with joy and happiness.

Jesus said, "I am the truth." The Source of all wisdom
is within you. If you want your life to have meaning and
purpose you must turn to your Father. To know Him and
His will for you is to make your human world more meaningful, pleasant, and enjoyable.

The I AM God in you is the way to life. Jesus said that
God within you is the Source of healing. This life force and
energy within us is never sick and it never ages. It seems to
because we have been taught that it does and we believe
that it does and therefore it manifests accordingly. We are
humanly more aware of life today. For the most part we
are free of many of the primitive superstitions about this
life force. Most do not believe that evil spirits make us
sick; they now believe it is germs. We don't perform religious rituals as a general rule trying to placate these spirits
even though we do try to placate God or coerce Him to
heal us. God's life within you and me and everyone is
already perfect. If we had a perfect consciousness or
perfect awareness of this life we would have perfect
health.

Is it difficult to follow in the way? Not really. It only
seems that way. All beginnings seem difficult and challenging and even scary. But when we accept the challenge
and grow in faith and trust and in the development of consciousness we make it pretty well. The strait way only
means living by principle. If we listen to the I AM God
and are obedient, we find that the strait way is a great
way, for it leads to life; it leads to mastery over the
physical.

Human needs are always filled when we follow the strait way. In another of His I AM statements Jesus said, "I am the bread of life; he who comes to me shall not hunger, and he who believes in me shall never thirst." (John 6:35) What a tremendous promise and statement! God not only will but can take care of you. Trusting Him relieves us of struggling and competing and striving. It makes us more creative and productive. The human part of us will be utterly amazed at what God can accomplish when we abide in the consciousness of His presence.

If you will let the Father work through you, you will discover that what you are called upon to do will not be work, but a joy.

A PRIME REQUIREMENT

A man was put in prison, convicted of a crime he did not commit. After many years the real criminal confessed. The man was set free. When talking to reporters about the experience he said, "I can never forgive them."

It would be quite a challenge to forgive in this circumstance. Even the most noble and religious person in human consciousness would find it difficult or practically impossible to do. And yet, forgiveness is a prime requirement for entering into a true relationship with God, conscious oneness with God. Forgiveness is a prime requirement for healing and many other human fulfillments.

How important was forgiveness in the teachings of Jesus? It would be in the top five if we were to number them in a sequential order. Just listen to these words of Jesus as recorded in Matthew 5:23 & 24: "If you are offering a gift at the altar, and there remember that your brother has something against you, leave your gift there before the altar and go; first be reconciled to your brother, and then come and offer your gift." The implication here is that before we can be receptive to God's guidance we must first be open and receptive in consciousness and this means willing to make amends. He is saying in so many words that we can't have a true prayer experience until there is a genuine and sincere effort to release any feelings of hate, resentment, or bitterness.

Jesus also stressed the importance of forgiveness in the Lord's Prayer. In Matthew 6:12 He says, "Forgive us our debts, as we also have forgiven our debtors." He is telling us that when we pray we should have already forgiven and we are asking God to forgive us to the same degree that we forgive others. If we set conditions for our forgiveness of others we are asking God to set the same conditions toward us. If we are reluctant and lukewarm we want God to be reluctant and lukewarm toward us.

He even went a step further and said, "If you forgive men their trespasses, your heavenly Father also will forgive you." (Matthew 6:14) And if we do not forgive, then the Father will not forgive us. The idea being brought out here is not that God doesn't want to, but that He can't. He can't express His love through us as forgiveness as long as we are holding unforgiving thoughts and feelings toward someone.

These statements on forgiveness by Jesus make us rather uncomfortable, because we feel the inadequacy of our human ability. We realize that to express forgiveness we must go beyond this human capacity.

Jesus set the example for forgiveness. He was unjustly accused and put in prison. His imprisonment was even more unjust than the example I mentioned, for that individual had quite a criminal record whereas Jesus had none. Jesus was eventually executed. He knew He was innocent of all the charges against Him. He was rejected by the masses, the very people he was seeking to help. He was rejected even by some of His closest friends and followers. He was ridiculed; they spit on Him; they beat Him; they tortured Him; and they mocked Him. Yet, even while on the cross He was able to say, "Father, forgive them, for they know not what they do."

Jesus knew they were hurting themselves more than they were hurting Him. In fact they were not hurting Him at all, not even physically. Jesus felt no pain, not even the pain of the spear that pierced His side. Jesus never suffered any physical pain from the beatings He was subjected to. We are gaining some objective proof of this today in the experiences of individuals who go through trying conditions, and yet they do not experience pain. There is the example of the soldier who stepped on a land mine in Vietnam. He was blown into the air; his right arm was severed along with his right leg. His left leg was almost severed and later had to be removed. He states that at that moment he felt peace. He saw them take his body from the battlefield to an Army hospital. All this time he was out of the body and did not experience any pain. Now if he, a human with little knowledge of how to control the physical body, can have an experience of this type and not experience pain, I am certain that Jesus the Master teacher could control His body experiences even better than this.

Jesus knew it was useless to resent or to hate those who were doing the negative things to Him. There would be no satisfaction, no relief in seeing his accusers punished. Yet that is exactly what the human wants when it is offended. On the human level we seem to think that if we only hold long enough to feelings of hate and resentment, we will gain some type of compensation; we will make someone else suffer and this will make us feel better. If we are to enter into a conscious relationship with God, however, we must come to grips with human offenses. We cannot let them simmer. I have known instances of individuals hating for years. In one case I know of, a man hated someone in his own family for over thirty years. Some people even hate others who are no longer living. What could be more useless than this!

How can we deal with this human tendency? It may be helpful to ask and answer this question, "What good does it do to hate anyone for any reason?" For example, the man I mentioned who was put in prison unjustly: what good will it do him not to forgive? The ones who had a part in putting him there may be dead or not even knowing anything about him any longer. They certainly won't be affected by his hate—only he will be affected by that. Therefore it will not do him one bit of good.

Hating or resenting doesn't make the one hating happy. Have you ever heard of such a thing as a "happy hater"? Really, when we stop to think about it we can't find one good reason to continue to hate, resent, or continue to hold a desire for revenge. Hate can't restore relationships. It can't undo what has been done. It can't even prevent the mistakes or injustices from happening again. If Americans had kept hating the Japanese for the Pearl Harbor incident, where would we be today?—no Datsuns, Toyotas, Hondas; no hi-fi stereo systems that many enjoy. There would be no harmonious relations with the people. But because there was the willingness to forgive, God's love has established a beautiful relationship.

Hating others is used as a national, political arouser. People have even been taught to hate in the name of religion. Hating evil will not dissolve it or exterminate it or necessarily protect one from its influence. Christians should really know this, for we have been taught to hate the evil and love the good, an impossibility. The conclusion therefore is this—it is totally and absolutely useless and futile to continue or even desire to continue in a consciousness of hate.

But what can we do about it? It seems that we can't help ourselves or stop it. When we try it seems we only repress it. Even getting angry doesn't help us get it out of our system. Yet we are told it is healthy to give vent to our anger as a good psychological release. However, we should note that continuing to express feelings of anger for any reason can have a very negative effect upon our physical system. It can affect our blood pressure and heart; acids secreted into the system can cause various forms of illness. So "lid-blowing" is not a practical solution.

The first step is that we must humanly come to the point where we can say to ourselves that we want to forgive, where we realize the necessity to do so, even if it seems that we may lose something such as money, influence, or reputation. We may be seething with hurt feelings and resentment and it may seem humanly impossible to say, "I forgive," but we must still say, "God, I want to forgive." If we can do this we have taken a great human step.

When Jesus said that an individual offering a gift should "go" and seek reconciliation before praying He did not mean that we would have to seek out the person. Reconciliation is something that takes place in consciousness. The other person may not be available or he may not want to forgive. The reconciliation doesn't mean the negative feelings are or will be dissolved at that moment. It only means that we humanly be willing to forgive.

Forgiveness is an expression of love that is above our human capacity to love. We can do some pretty noble and wonderful things with human love but forgiveness is not one of them. When we are willing to let go, a wonderful thing will happen in us. We will experience an inrush of God's love so powerful that it will forgive through us. With this expression of unconditional love there will be a feeling of peace and harmony that we have never known before. This will happen whether the circumstances that caused the disturbed feelings, or the persons who had a part in arousing them in us, are there or not, or whether they have changed or not.

Along with this feeling of mental and emotional peace, there will be a tremendous feeling of relief—no more carrying of the burden of hate. When this flooding of the consciousness with love takes place we won't even be concerned about whether the other person will get away with what he or she has done to us. We certainly do not have to wait for a favorable response from another person or from the world before we can experience this peace of forgiveness and release. In this consciousness of God's forgiving love we are also free of self-condemnation and all feelings of guilt. We are at peace with ourselves about ourselves.

We don't have to wait for social justice to take place. That may be a long time in coming. People have been waiting for that throughout Old Testament times, New Testament times, and all the centuries since. We don't have to wait for equal opportunities to come our way, for we will have such a consciousness of oneness with God that we will know that no one can keep our good from us. God is the Source and when we are consciously one with the Source we have peace and security and fulfillment. Even if someone doesn't forgive us and continues to hate us, we will still have our peace. That person may not, but we will.

In our moments of prayer we should ask, "God, let your forgiving love express through me. I want to forgive and I do not set any conditions. Let your love wipe the slate of consciousness clean." The ultimate would be to rise in consciousness to the point where we can declare along with Jesus, right in the face of the most negative condition or experience, "Father, forgive them, for they know not what they do."

"BEHOLD I SEND MY MESSENGER"

When some phenomenon occurs that we do not understand, we usually give some religious or pseudo-scientific explanation for its occurrence. In ancient times when a person became ill it was believed that that illness was due to an evil spirit. Healing took place when the spirit was cast out. The ancients also believed that God was up in the sky and that he had messengers or angels that delivered His messages to prophets and messiahs. There are no angels as they have been pictured, beings with wings on their backs.

An example of Old Testament explanations of the phenomenon of God guiding an individual is contained in a passage in Exodus where God speaks to Moses and says, "Behold, I send an angel before you, to guard you on the way and to bring you to the place which I have prepared." (Ex. 23:20) The people, under Moses' leadership, had just left their Egyptian bondage. They were very discouraged. They did not know how to live in freedom and were ready to turn back to Egypt and become slaves again. But Moses had the vision of a Promised Land and God was assuring him of success if the people would only follow the messenger.

It wasn't going to be an easy trip from Sinai to the Promised Land. The people were given some instructions. They were to listen to and be obedient to the messenger or angel. "Do not rebel against Him." (Ex. 23:21) If they would listen, then all their enemies on the way would be defeated. They were not to bow down to them or their gods, nor serve them. They were not to do according to their works. The instruction was very plain—"You shall serve the Lord your God." (Ex. 23:26)

The Lord would supply their needs, even in the desert where it seemed impossible to have an adequate supply of bread and water. He would heal them and bless them with long life, something desired by all.

They were cautioned about expecting immediate results—"I will not drive them out before you in one year." (Ex. 23:20) In this day and age we are used to expecting "instant" everything, not realizing that it is "little by little I will drive them out from before you, until you are increased and possess the land." (Ex. 23:30) It takes much prayer and study to build the consciousness through which God can work to provide for all our needs. They were warned that "If you serve their gods it will surely be a snare to you." (Ex. 23:33) These gods are the outer things we often worship which we think will make us happy, successful, or that will even heal us. When we follow the guidance of the inner messenger we find that we become involved in life in a very different manner. Instead of seeking things from the world to make us happy we seek to give something to the world as an expression of our inner happiness. When we express from this level of consciousness God provides for our needs without our making the seeking of things the object of our existence.

None of us is in his right place. Oh, in metaphysical terminology we always say that everyone is in his right place according to his consciousness. This is so. But we are not in the place where we should be, the Promised Land, the full conscious realization of our oneness with God. Some are not even out of Egyptian slavery, the bondage of human consciousness. Some are still slaving away trying to satisfy their sense demands.

However, some of us are on the Sinai to Promised Land trip. Moses received the revelation of the Law on Mt. Sinai. This means that we have come to realize that this is a universe of law, that nothing happens by chance, accident, or the whims of a fickle god. What a relief it is to realize that God does not play favorites. I may not always know or even understand why some things happen in my life but I can be sure that when the law is applied as it should be, only good will be the result. We live in a society with many laws. We believe that if people would live by these laws we would have peace and harmony. But not everyone wants to live by the law. We search for ways around the law, universal law. We do something we know we should not do and when we get some negative result we want to find a way to deal with that without giving up the negative cause. For example, we may eat something that we know we should not eat. When we get the upset stomach we then take an Alka Seltzer or something of that nature to deal with the upset stomach. These human attempts to circumvent the law are futile.

Many people believe they can think, feel, or do anything they want to do and not have to deal with any consequences, if they can get away with it in the society in which they live. They fail to realize that there is only one society, God's society, and it is governed by universal and unchanging laws. What we sow we reap, not only of the negative but also of the good.

In this state of awareness of God as universal law we are not fully aware of the great power of God for good. We have times of trusting and times of doubting. We have moments of communion with Him but we also have many more when we feel separate and alone. Even when we know intellectually that we are one with Him, nevertheless we feel alone. However, in the moments of communion we are inspired and told by His messenger or angel what we should do or not do to make things right in our lives. We are assured that the messenger will go before us to guide and prepare the way for us.

I am sure you have had the experience of following

God's guidance and discovering that as you went forward it seemed that someone was going before you and preparing the way. People that you thought might be against you now cooperate with you.

In the Gospel of Mark the messenger has been interpreted to be John the Baptist. He did come, bringing the message that the coming of Jesus would bring an even greater message than that of John's. We have been looking for the coming of a Messiah as a personality. The Hebrews expected a Messiah as a king. The real messenger is not a personality, it is the Lord within you. There are persons such as Jesus and others who can help us on this plane and there are others who can help us on other planes of existence, but they can only do so much. Jesus said our greatest help would come when we turned to the Father within us. Then He would guide us into all the truth. He would take care of us, provide for our needs, and heal us of our wounds. We may think of those around us as angels because of their great help, but we should realize that our greatest help comes from God, from the direct inspiration from the Source within us. Remember the words to Moses, "You shall serve the Lord your God." You shall follow the inner guidance, not the free advice of some friend, relative, or other acquaintance.

The guidance may be challenging but it always leads to greater good. We are not to serve the gods of the human personality, the intellect, and the senses. Those gods promise so much and deliver so little. When we follow the messenger of God, wonderful things begin to happen. Seemingly insurmountable problems are overcome. It seems that doors open before us with little or no human effort. It is like walking through the doors operated by an "electric eye" at the supermarket. Things and persons who seemed to be against us begin to work with us or leave us alone. If they do work with us, they do it without any "armbending" tactics on our part. The messenger, the power of God expressing through our consciousness, may open the way for a loan to be approved to buy a home, or for us to get a job, or to meet the person who will complement some desire for love and companionship. When we have to make a major move or change in our lives it is reassuring to know that the power of God can and will go before us to prepare the way.

This is true not only for the human experiences of life but it is also true in moving on from the consciousness of law to the supreme consciousness of love. The development of that consciousness comes "little by little." It comes with persistent seeking and putting to work what we know to be true. Living in harmony with the universal laws of life becomes very easy when it is done from the level of unconditional love. As the Bible tells us, "Love overcomes all things" and "Love is the fulfilling of the law." It is the fulfilling of the law in its highest and the blessings are beyond our human imaginative comprehension.

JOYOUS EXPECTATIONS

When a person is expecting something and has his mind already made up as to how his expectation should be fulfilled, it is quite difficult to reach him with another view. In fact, in many cases it is practically impossible.

Jesus had this difficulty when He endeavored to communicate to His disciples and the people His idea of the Messiah. It seemed at first that He had made it, for they accepted Him with joyous expectations on Palm Sunday. But their joy on Sunday turned to hate and total rejection within a few days. The human mind, when disappointed, can become very vicious.

Jesus had spent a great deal of His time teaching in Galilee and other areas. He knew it would take a long time for the full impact of what He was saying to take effect. His disciples who were with Him all the time had difficulty grasping His ideas. Some never quite made it. Now, near the end of His time on earth He was about to give them His greatest demonstration of truth teaching in the events beginning with Palm Sunday and ending with His resurrection on Easter morning.

According to His disciple, John, Jesus was in the Jerusalem area about six days before He made His outward move. No doubt He was laying the groundwork with others who would take part in this great drama of life. These events didn't just happen, they were planned. The donkey wasn't at its post just by accident. Jesus also needed a place to have His final meal and a tomb to be used after the crucifixion.

The first step in this drama of eternal life was to make it

very clear who the Messiah was, and what kind of a Messiah He was to be. The people were expecting the Messiah to come and deliver them. They expected him to be a military commander like their great king David. They expected him to defeat the Romans and reestablish the great kingdom of Israel. This was the dominant theme.

There were many zealots who were always ready for a fight to the death if some Messiah would only come along and lead them in battle with the help of God's army of angels. The people were always looking for signs of the coming of the Messiah. John the Baptist raised their hopes when he proclaimed to be the "voice crying in the wilderness." Many felt the time had arrived and God was about to intervene in history and destroy the Romans for them.

Now Jesus came along and had to set them straight. But they didn't want to be set straight. They wanted the Messiah to come as they expected Him to come and to be the type of Messiah they were expecting Him to be. Jesus decided to act out the Messianic idea in a simple way. Maybe this would open a way into their closed minds and they would begin to realize that the Messiah was going to be something quite different.

On Palm Sunday morning He got His disciples together for the trip into Jerusalem. They were scared to go to the city for there was so much opposition to Jesus from the religious leaders and many of the people. But they probably thought that the time had arrived and Jesus was about to begin the great liberating event.

They stopped at the Mt. of Olives. The Messiah was expected to show up here. Things were looking good. However instead of sending for a war horse Jesus sent them for a donkey. This was a modifying clue about the Messiah but they missed it. The prophecy had said, "Rejoice greatly, O daughter of Zion! Shout aloud, O daughter of Jerusalem! Lo, your king comes to you; triumphant and victorious is he, humble and riding on a donkey, on a colt the foal of a donkey." (Zech. 9:9) They probably were thinking, "When He gets into the city, then He will lead the attack."

The disciples found the donkey, gave the password "The Lord has need of him" to the owners, and brought the donkey to Jesus. Then the procession began, from the Mt. of Olives into the city of Jerusalem. The disciples were excited by now and as they went along they picked up many followers. By the time they reached the city they were really worked up and were shouting, "Hosanna, blessed is he that comes in the name of the Lord. Blessed is the kingdom that cometh, the kingdom of our father David: Hosanna in the highest." (Mark 11:9–10) When Jesus arrived in the city He went to the Temple and began cleaning out the moneychangers and animals. This was quite a shock. They thought he would be cleaning out the Romans. They had been shouting "Hosanna," which means, save us. But this wouldn't save them. Jesus wanted to save them but not on their terms, for their terms couldn't save them even if a military commander had come to lead them in battle.

If Jesus returned today, He would have the same problem. The masses would want Him to come as the Messiah the way they are expecting Him to come. But He would have to say to them, "It can't be that way." They expected the coming of the Messiah to be a time of great victory. Jesus couldn't lead them to victory on a donkey. Besides, he kept talking about dying, and telling them the Temple and the city would be destroyed. This was another shock to them.

The Messiah has come already. He has been received by some. Others have received Him but have also rejected Him a number of times. But he is patient and not upset over rejection. He waits until we are ready and willing. The key words are "ready" and "willing." He will come and lead us through the crucifixion on to the resurrection.

The word Messiah comes from the Hebrew and means "that which is to save." Christ is the Greek form of the same idea. That which is to save you and me is God; it is God within you and God within me. It is the same God that was in Jesus. It is the God He referred to as "Father." He referred to those who were aware of the Father within as "sons of God." Like Jesus, they would have a mature understanding of their relationship with God within. In metaphysical terminology everyone is said to be a son of God. It should more properly be stated that everyone is a child of God, for not everyone understands the significance of the relationship. A child does not understand the full meaning of its relationship with its parents.

The coming of the Messiah is the coming into consciousness of a genuine realization of our oneness with God. This realization comes, not with a big spectacular display of outer earthly phenomena or psychological phenomena. The coming of the Messiah is very subtle. It is quite different from what we expect it to be. He comes as a thief in the night, very quietly, not announcing Himself with great outer signs.

He will come, not as a king, taking control and demanding obedience to His will. Our human will must volunteer to follow Him; He will never force us. We can reject Him and many times do so before we get around to realizing that He is wiser than we are. The human part of us knows so much and expects so much and is reluctant to let go of or change these expectations.

When He comes He will bring peace, but it won't be by changing people, governments, or economies. He will not lead us in an attack on these outer Romans; He will lead us in cleansing our inner Temple, our mind. He will help us to cast out our mistaken religious, theological, social, cultural, and other beliefs that are stumbling blocks to the development of the "kingdom of God" consciousness.

At first it may seem that we are headed for total defeat. but if we will only remain faithful to Him He will bring us to a greater victory than the one we had anticipated. He will lead us to victory over sickness and lack. He will take care of us and provide for all our needs. But this provision can only be on His terms. It will not be through violence and taking things from others. He doesn't have to destroy any of our so-called enemies. If we look to Him we will never have to look to another human being again for our happiness and security, for we will be secure in Him. He can fulfill all needed expectations joyously and abundantly.

THE GREAT VICTORY

Jesus died on the cross about 3 p.m. on Friday. Joseph of Arimathea asked for permission from Pilate to take the body down and place it in his private tomb. He wanted this completed before the Sabbath began, which was 6 p.m. So he had about three hours to do it. According to all Gospel records, Jesus was in the tomb until just before dawn on Sunday morning. This is a maximum of 38 hours, possibly less, that Jesus could have spent in the tomb. The hours did cover portions of three days, and this was a customary way of computing time. However, He was not in the tomb three days and three nights; only two nights.

Sunday morning is exciting and joyous news to us, for we know what happened and how events turned out. The women going to the tomb didn't know. In fact they expected to find the body of Jesus in the tomb. They asked the question among themselves, "Who will roll away the stone?" They had purchased special ointments to give his body a permanent burial.

The Gospels of Mark, Matthew, and Luke have three women going to the tomb. There were two Marys and either a Salome or Joanna. Mark states that a "young man in white" was in the empty tomb when they arrived. Matthew says there was an angel sitting on the stone outside the tomb. Luke says two men in dazzling apparel were in the tomb. All three agree that these individuals spoke to the women telling them that Jesus had risen from the dead and that they should go and tell his disciples.

Now the Gospel of John tells quite a different story. It seems that John tells the history of the incident with a view toward a deeper spiritual meaning. He says that Mary Magdalene came to the tomb before dawn, "while it was yet dark." She finds the tomb open and empty. She immediately runs to find Peter to tell him, "They have taken away the Lord out of the tomb and we know not where they have laid Him." (John 20:2) John was with Peter and when they heard this they began running to the tomb to see for themselves. John says he outran Peter and got to the tomb first. He stops at the entrance, not wanting to become defiled according to religious law. When Peter arrives, he doesn't hesitate; he goes right on in. When John sees this example of courage over tradition he too enters the tomb. They see the linen cloths lying in the tomb but that is all. There are no men or angels in white to tell them Jesus rose from the dead. Satisfied that the body must have been stolen they walk out of the tomb, disappointed, and leave.

Mary remained outside the tomb crying. She not only believed Jesus was still dead but that someone had stolen the body, or at least put it somewhere else. After a time she looked into the tomb and it was then that she saw two angels. They ask her why she is weeping and she repeats what she told Peter and John. Before the angels can answer, she notices someone behind her. This person also asks her why she is crying. She thinks he is a gardener and asks if he knows where the body of Jesus has been laid: "Sir, if thou hast borne him hence, tell me where thou hast laid him, and I will take him away." (John 20:15) Jesus just speaks her name, "Mary." The love and compassion in His voice must have broken through her negative mental obsession, for she then recognizes Him and says, "Rabboni." Was she ever startled to realize it was Jesus and that He was very much alive! He tells her to go and tell the others that He is risen and that He will soon ascend to His Father. Also that He will appear to them soon. So she goes with the joyous news as Jesus disappears.

Why is the resurrection so important to us? It seems impossible. Some believe it and there are probably many who do not believe it. After all it was Jesus' death that became more important in the Christian theology of salvation—He died to save them. What is the ascension? Do we really believe in it, that Jesus had a physical body while he was here but that when He left, He took it with Him? When Jesus said, "Follow Me," did He mean for us to go all the way, including the resurrection and the ascension? When He said, "The works I do, ye shall do also, and greater works than these shall ye do," did He mean to include the resurrection and ascension? When He said, "If you can believe, all things are possible," did He mean the resurrection and ascension also? Or was Jesus "talking through his hat"? Have we just failed to grasp the full significance of His message to us? If we are to understand what He is trying to communicate we must face the difficult questions. We are approaching the dawn of a new day in our search for truth. In this search we must realize that Easter is more than a time to enjoy a beautiful spring day. The ideas related to Easter, the resurrection and ascension, come before us with regularity. What are we doing with them? Do we really believe there is something to them?

When we begin seeking the answers to these ideas of life, we will discover that life takes on a totally new appearance for us. It doesn't change as much as we do. We discover that life becomes more than the seeking of a variety of pleasant physical and sensory experiences. We also discover that spiritual sensation is far greater than physical sensation. We begin to realize the magnitude and immensity of life. A number of years ago, we reflected our shortsightedness as a nation when we accepted the slogan "The Last Frontier." We were a great nation and had accomplished many wonderful things in the name of science, including going to the moon. Now we know better; there is no end to new frontiers. We are only just now playing around in space. There is far more that we don't know and can't do. Yes, we rejoice in our accomplishments, but we should remember they are only meagre right now. We are only just playing around wtih the so-called frontiers of the mind. We are fascinated with the phenomena we can produce and are trying to find ways to use this power to a greater personal degree, to have better health, more money, and more control over our physical lives.

Progress seems slow and it probably is, for we are slow to accept new ideas, especially when they are challenging. If we were to go back in history to an imaginary session and tell a group of people in the horse and buggy days about our present accomplishments and tell them these things were on the way, they would probably not believe them. Ideas about life that Jesus tried to communicate almost 2,000 years ago were hard to believe then and they are still hard to believe. We want proof. We want intellectual reasons and explanations based on laws we already know about. If we had that kind of proof we would be doing those things. We will never understand the great truths of life completely from just an intellectual analysis and search.

John, in his Gospel, is trying to help us realize this. When we consider his version, we find he is telling us more about the resurrection and ascension, and about where we will find our proof that these great ideas are true. In John's version, Jesus appeared first to Mary Magdalene. Why not to Peter and Paul while they were there? If Jesus had the ability to appear and disappear at will, why did he wait until they left and then appear to Mary? Why didn't Jesus first appear to His mother? Why not to the ones who were His close followers, the twelve? Why to this woman with the harlot background? Why to a woman first?

The intellect will probably never be satisfied with any explanation about the resurrection and ascension. There are many, many theories to prove and many to disprove them, none in a conclusive or satisfactory way. Some use the Bible to prove the resurrection is true, but this isn't proof to satisfy a searching scientist. Some are excited about the finding of the Shroud as scientific evidence, but that isn't conclusive evidence. It doesn't prove it was Jesus' body, and even if it was, it doesn't prove Jesus rose from the dead. It could mean the women found a dead Jesus and decided to wrap the body in fresh garments when they anointed it and then told the story of the resurrection. Some Christian Bible scholars believe the resurrection was only a resurrection in the minds of his followers and not a factual experience.

The only way the human part of us will ever be satisfied is through revealed truth and that is an intuitive experience, a non-intellectual experience. It comes through much meditation and inner seeking and a willingness to accept what the real truth is.

Mary Magdalene, in John's telling of the story, represents the human soul which has had many "harlot experiences" with outer things and has found them lacking, and now has turned to the seeking of the truth. Jesus appearing to her first means that intuitive or spiritual truth that reveals the truth about the resurrection and ascension is first made evident to us through the feeling nature as a non-intellectual experience. When that takes place we *know* the resurrection and ascension are true and we do not need any outer proof. Furthermore, we know that they are true not only for Jesus but that they are true as possibilities for us. We know Jesus meant what He said in those statements of His that I have already quoted.

When this inner, illuminating experience takes place, our intellectual capacities—Peter and John—can accept these great ideas as possibilities even though at the moment they seem so impossible for us to accomplish. We know and can accept that they are now our true spiritual goals that will be accomplished when we have fully established a conscious relationship with God. The human soul is quickened by this great idea and the journey toward achieving the great victory over death and rebirth either begins or is intensified. We begin to expand our thinking about life and realize there is more to it than an endless round of death and rebirth.

The great victory is never achieved by seeking only outer improvements. We use what we know and what science has been able to accomplish and we give thanks for these blessings. However, we do not stop there. We continue to press on, as Paul states it, to the high calling of God in Christ Jesus. We press on in our times of meditation and study in seeking a conscious oneness with God.

Jesus gave to us a statement that we should take into our minds and hearts and cherish with all the love and appreciation and feeling we can muster. It is a statement to remind us of these great ideas that He taught. This is the statement: "I AM THE RESURRECTION AND THE LIFE. . . . WHOEVER LIVES AND BELIEVES IN ME SHALL NEVER DIE." He isn't talking about some so-called spiritual death. Many are dead spiritually who think they are alive; they just don't know how dead they are with their limited views about Jesus and what He taught. He is talking about the resurrection and the ascension. After all, God's will for us is life. He is the God of the living, those seeking to express as He created them to express in a body that is free of all limitation, a body that never again experiences physical death.

A statement of the ultimate great victory was made by Paul in one of his better moments when he said, "The last enemy that shall be overcome is death." And if I may paraphrase another of His statements, "Christ in you is your hope of achieving this great victory." How long will it take? Who knows? What difference does it make? It has already been too long. As humans we have been occupying planet earth for thousands of years and no doubt have had many physical incarnations at various times throughout this period. There have been some who have already made the resurrection in consciousness that leads to the ascension experience and they are no longer in bondage to this earthly, human cycle of life. It is up to each individual. The more open and receptive and willing we are to let the Spirit of God grow and express through us, the sooner we too shall live as Jesus lives and as many others live, for we will have achieved the great victory.

"NOT MY WILL"

Jesus said He came to do the will of God and to teach us how to do the will of God. He said, "My food is to do the will of him who sent me and to accomplish his work." (John 4:34) On another occasion He said, "I can do nothing on my own authority; as I hear, I judge; and my judgment is just, because I seek not my own will but the will of him who sent me." (John 5:30)

On the eternal pathway of life that we are all traveling we all must come to the point where we must make a big decision, on both human and spiritual levels. That decision is this: shall I do things God's way or shall I continue to do them my own personal way? After many failures and many frustrating efforts to achieve happiness, success, health, or some other good, the human part of us realizes, as Jesus said, "I can do nothing on my own authority." So the human part of us has to decide whether we shall live on the personal level or the spiritual level; whether we shall seek to live according to principles of truth or according to our human way.

Jesus expressed this making of a decision as "not my will, but thine be done." In the Lord's Prayer He gave us an example of how we should pray: "Thy will be done on earth as it is in heaven." He knew that only in following God's guidance would we ever know the joy He knew and have the power, mastery, and dominion that He had.

It is not an easy decision for the human part of us to make. We have so many wonderful plans that we are convinced will make life so much more pleasant if God would only fulfill them, and we are reluctant to give them up. We think we know how our problems should be solved and sometimes individuals spend a great deal of their prayer time trying to convince God to go along with them. We also have some cherished beliefs, secular and religious, that are so sacred to us that we hold to them tenaciously. We have relationships and other human attachments to persons and things of the world and we may find it very challenging to be willing to let them go and say, "Not my will but thine be done." To be willing to put all these and other human desires aside is asking a lot from our human point of view but it is something that must be done.

Being willing to give up our human point of view and human attachments doesn't mean we give up all human living and go and live in a desert. Jesus didn't do that. What it means is simply this, that we be willing to give up whatever is necessary in order to follow the guidance of God, God's will. On the human level we think many things are necessary to our happiness and well-being that are not essential at all.

What is God's will? Let me assure you that it is not to make your life miserable but more wonderful. God's will is not to take away from you but to add greater blessings to you. God's will is never any form of limitation, never sickness or accident; never poverty; and never, never, violent and destructive weather. God never punishes. He never chastises, even the ones He loves, and that includes everyone. God doesn't have to do negative things to us to see how we will respond, for He knows us better than we know ourselves and therefore He only has to love us and be willing to help us. That is what His will is—the help that, if followed, will add blessings far beyond our greatest expectations.

The human mind may cry out and ask, "Why or what causes all these unpleasant things to happen in my life and in the world?" They happen because the human doesn't know how to live. Not knowing causes us to make many mistakes that have undesirable consequences. What happens when a person who doesn't know how to swim falls into water over his head? Not knowing how to swim, he drowns. Not knowing how to make decisions based on principles of truth, God's will, causes us to make decisions based on appearances, and that can be tragic. Not knowing how to love will cause problems. Not knowing how to stand firm in faith when confronted with problems that seem overwhelming can cause difficulties for us. Knowing how to do something makes an individual a master. Jesus was a master of His life, for He knew His oneness with God and was always shown how to meet the challenges that arose. He was even able to control the weather.

At our present level of understanding we do not see the relationship and influence of consciousness on our environment, but it is there. Violence in consciousness begets violence in the earth and in the personal life of the individual. Harmony, love, and truth in consciousness beget harmony and protection in mind, emotions, and experience.

Letting go of personal, human desires opens the way for understanding and mastery. Desiring to do God's will adds power and dominion to our lives. God knows where we stand in consciousness. He knows what misconceptions must be released before we can accept some of the basic and higher truths about life. He knows what attachments must be released, what relationships must be terminated or which ones we should establish. He knows what we need to do in order to grow in spiritual consciousness. He knows what we need to learn in order that we may be more richly fed and prospered.

Making a commitment to work with God may entail the accepting of some challenges we might not prefer, for they may not seem to offer fame, prestige, or fortune. However, when we accept God's guidance we find that fame, prestige, and worldly accumulations are not necessary to happiness, a feeling of security, peace of mind, and many other desirable qualities of mind, heart, and experience. We also have another very pleasant surprise. When we get to the point where we can sincerely say, "Not my will, but thine be done," we find many "things" are added that we had not even expected. Relationships are added that are right for us. Supply for our needs comes forth to care for our human needs.

When we develop a degree of consciousness through which God can work, then even other works may be asked of us. When Jesus came to this earth plane of existence to undertake the challenge of proving to humanity the power of God working through individual consciousness, He was selected, not because God wanted to punish Him or make Him suffer, but because Jesus had the consciousness through which the glory, power, and majesty of God could express. If you were the owner of a business and one of your companies was having trouble, you would send your most capable worker there to do what was necessary to make the company a success. Jesus said, "I came down from heaven, not to do my own will, but the will of him who sent me." (John 6:35) He came from a higher level of conscious existence to this human, three dimensional level to show us the power of God, to show and to teach us how to live in harmony with the universal, eternal laws of life.

If we are to get in tune with God so that He may work His marvelous works through us, then willingness to accept whatever may be revealed is important. The affirmation, "Not my will but thine be done," should not be said with negative expectations but with very positive ones. We don't seek to do God's will in order to get things, but when we do what He guides us to do, many wonderful things are added. When we are doing what He guides us to do we experience greater joy than the joy of just getting some "thing."

"A NEW COMMANDMENT"

The first time Jesus gave the new commandment to the disciples was at the last supper. He had already told Judas to leave and be about his business. Jesus knew what Judas was up to, the betrayal that would lead to His arrest and the crucifixion. It was at this time that He said, "A new commandment I give to you, that you love one another; even as I have loved you." (John 13:34)

On the way to the Garden of Gethsemane after the supper, Jesus elaborated further on this idea of love. He said, "As the Father has loved me, so have I loved you; abide in my love." (John 15:9) Jesus was conscious of God's love for Him, the magnitude of that love and how far superior it was to the ordinary human expression of love. He also said, "These things I have spoken to you, that my joy may be in you, and that your joy may be full." (John 15:11) Keep in mind as you read these words that Jesus was on the way to being arrested and crucified and He still maintains that His heart was filled with joy. He also repeats the idea of the new commandment, saying, "that you love one another as I have loved you." (John 15:12)

The human part of us might say, "It is impossible to love someone that is going to do what Judas did." Humanly, it is impossible to love to that high degree. It will take more than a human realization and expression of love to love as Jesus loved; it will take a spiritual realization of this great divine quality. It will take a realization of God's love for us and a willingness to let God's love express through us.

Did you know that no one has ever loved you as much as God loves you? Even your parents in their better moments have not loved you as much. Wives and husbands haven't been able to love as much as God loves. No friend has ever loved you as much as God loves you, even if that friend has given his life for you.

Most of us haven't even realized that God loves us and because of this we find it difficult to comprehend the nature of this great quality of love and to express it. We have been led to believe that God loves us as a human might love us. We have thought that God loves us only when we are good and when we are in His grace. We have thought that God withholds His love when we do something that is wrong. We have even gone so far as to think that this great and wonderful God of love has had the imagination to create a place of eternal torture and suffering for those He decides not to love and forgive. Our human concept of God's love has been very limited and negative.

Are you ready now for a new statement of how much God loves you, me, and everyone? It will be shocking to the human mind to hear how great His love for us really is. His love for you is unconditional. This means that He loves you just as you are. You do not have to be what we humans call "good." You do not even have to be "saved." Even when we are in the very act of violating universal laws of life, God loves us. Even while the murderer is committing the most brutal murder, God loves both equally. That is really difficult to comprehend, much less to feel, for the human part of us would feel rage, anger, and even hate. It would also have a strong desire to punish the one who commits the crime as severely as the one who was the victim.

Can you see now why we must rise above our human concept of love? God loves you and me even if we do not know it. Even in our very human moments of anger at God for what we think of as His lack of interest, help, and concern, He loves us. His love for you will never change. There isn't anything that you can do or not do that will change His love for you or even the intensity of that love. God understands us, our human limitations and our human responses to life's problems and challenges. That is why He is trying to help us through His love, to lift us up to a higher realization of His love so that we can know and feel the joy that Jesus knew. Remember, Jesus expressed the idea of His joy on the way to the Garden; even though He knew He would be arrested there and later crucified, He still said, "These things I have spoken to you, that my joy may be in you, and that your joy may be full." (John 15:11)

Even when we have impoverished ourselves in riotous living, God loves us and still provides for us as He can. When we return to Him after an ordeal or many ordeals of human living we find the welcome mat out as the lost son discovered when he returned to his father's house. The son thought his father might reject him as a son so he had planned to ask for a servant's job. Even as a servant he would be better off than he was. We are like the son; we think God is thinking toward us in a human way and all the time God isn't thinking that way at all. The son was greatly surprised when the father rushed out to welcome him back home and gave him a new robe, put a ring on his finger, sandals on his feet, and gave orders to prepare a feast. We too are greatly surprised when we return to God and find that we are fully restored without the need for compensation or penalty.

The human finds this difficult to comprehend and accept. The human wants to punish all violations. It tries to be generous and make the punishment fit the crime. It can't see that the one committing the crime is already suffering greatly. What greater suffering and misery can there be than to experience the emptiness of not knowing God! Without the consciousness of God and His love for us there is no joy, no happiness, no hope or expectation of mastery and control of life and its many experiences. Instead, the individual, striving to overcome that emptiness, resorts to further degrading acts that even intensify the soul's misery. God's love doesn't seek to add to the misery of the individual but to lift him out of it all.

God's love is free. No price has to be paid by you or by anyone else in order for you to know, feel, and experience His love. And if you can accept it, God doesn't require the price of an innocent victim, as we have thought Jesus to be, in order to love us or restore us in the consciousness of His love. God has never required animals to be sacrificed though at one time humans thought God did. His love is given freely to all, saint and sinner alike, and it is given to the same degree. He doesn't love saints more than He loves sinners; He loves both equally. When His love is accepted it lifts us above all compensation of a negative kind. Living without the awareness of God produces its own misery and limitations.

In the awareness of God we are set free. Even if for the moment we are in some human bondage we still have peace, security and the joy of knowing that full restoration will take place. We know that as consciousness is transformed through a greater realization of the power of love, the outer world will have to change and no one will be able to prevent these changes for good.

How can we love to this high level? Not by charity, though when one loves he will be even more generous. But his generosity will be from a higher level of love. It will not seek recognition or rewards. Its reward is the privilege and the opportunity to love and to share. We can't humanly make ourselves love. We can humanly decide that we would like to be more loving and that is a human step in the right direction. The human part of us will have to come to grips with the realization that expressing love to the degree that Jesus suggested is going to be very challenging. There will be a crucifixion. The human will have to give up its pet prejudices, its resentments, hates, and its desires for revenge.

We will also have to spend many hours thinking about and meditating upon the idea of love as a spiritual quality. We won't do it in one five-minute meditation. And we will not do it in one day. It will take many, many hours and many, many days and years. We will have to persistently seek to prepare ourselves to be channels for a greater expression of love. In the beginning it will flow with a trickle, but even that trickle will transform us, our lives, and our relationships. It will be a great step just for the human part of us to realize that it is more rewarding to love than to be loved. As we grow in this new consciousness of love we will be free of the human responses and the human feelings about love. No longer will there be a need or desire to love for gain or reward or benefit or even pleasure. We will have discovered that loving is its own reward, its only benefit and pleasure and, as Jesus said, "Joy that is made full."

"TO THEM THAT HATH"

During the last week of His ministry on earth, Jesus told his disciples several parables so that the teaching about the kingdom of God would remain with them until enlightenment came for them and for others. One of these parables is called the Parable of the Talents. A variation of this parable was told by Jesus on other occasions and you might want to read them. The basic idea and theme to be discussed is contained as a conclusion in all three of these parables. The first is the Parable of the Sower and it is recorded in three Gospels: Mark 4:1–25; Matthew 13:1–23; Luke 8:4–18. The Parable of the Pounds is recorded in Luke 19:11–27. The Parable of the Talents that will be used in this discussion is recorded in Matthew 25:14–29.

The coming of the Messiah and the kingdom of God would be like a man going into another country who called his servants to take care of some of his money. To the first servant he gave five talents; to the second two talents; to the third he gave one talent. He then went on his journey. The first and second servants invested their money and increased it one hundred percent. The third servant buried his because he was afraid of his master. When the master returned he asked for an accounting. The first one told him he now had ten talents and he was praised for his wise use of the money. The second told his master he had four talents. He also was praised and the two of them were told that they would be "set over many things." In the Parable of the Pounds in Luke's Gospel they were put over ten cities. When the third servant told his master that he had buried his money for safekeeping, he was rebuked by his master and his one talent was taken from him and given to the one who had ten. As a conclusion to the parable Jesus said, "For to every one who has will more be given, and he will have abundance; but from him who has not, even what he has will be taken away." (Mat. 25:29)

Some of those who heard the Parable of the Pounds objected to what the master had done in taking away from the servant who had not increased his money and giving that money to the one who had the most. They thought this was not fair to take from one who had little and to give to one who already had much. But it was done anyway and it was after this that Jesus made the same statement that those who have will have more and those who do not have will lose what they do have. When we consider this parable from a human point of view it does seem unfair and unjust and unkind and unmerciful. The human would take from the one who had made money and give it to the one who had made none because of his fear. However, when we consider the mystical idea that Jesus is conveying to us we realize that this is based on principle and is not only fair and just but in truth is kind and merciful and good.

Naturally the question we would ask is, "To them that hath what?" What is this something that if one has it he will have more and abundance and if he does not have it, he will lose what he does possess? Is it the ability to make wise investments? I think not. Is it the knowledge of the mental law of mind action? This seems to work pretty well for one can increase his material possessions to a degree. Or is it a knowledge of the law that states, "Use is the law of increase"? Physical exercise is based on this principle and it seems to work. But it is really none of these things.

The mystical idea is simply this: "To those who have the consciousness of the inner Presence of God, they will have more abundance. Those who do not have this consciousness will lose what they do have." If we have this

God-awareness, not only will the outer part of our lives be increased but there will be a great increase in inner blessings—peace of mind, true security, faith, confidence, and all the other dynamic qualities we long to have, including a true awareness of love and the ability to express it unconditionally.

On the human level of thought we think that we need many outer things to be healthy, prosperous, happy, and successful. And because of this view we expect our good to come from people, governments, organizations, relatives, or other channels. An individual living in this very human consciousness will often do many things seeking to get what he thinks is rightfully his. If he can't get it from the rich he will try the government. If he can't get his good from these channels he may, in desperation, lie, steal, or cheat trying to get more abundance. Little does he realize that these negative efforts are doomed to failure. Even if he gets something, he will lose it.

However, when one has the consciousness of the inner Presence of God, this consciousness will manifest what he needs. If he needs money it will be provided. If he needs food, that will be provided. If he needs healing, that will come forth. This doesn't mean that all this will drop out of the sky. It simply means that in some way, somehow, God will work through the consciousness of the individual to provide for all the individual's needs. This will be done even when it seems impossible to do according to the appearances.

In the Parable of the Sower Jesus went into even more detail saying that some would reap thirty, some sixty, and some a hundredfold. Not everyone has the same degree of consciousness of God. Jesus had the 100 per cent. Some in the parable had none. A small degree of awareness will do more than the greatest human effort.

Our human mind would ask the question, "Is it really that simple?" The answer is, yes. We have been taught that life must be a struggle. Without the consciousness of the inner Presence of God it is not only a struggle but a losing battle. Even if life lasts a long time it seems that one continues to lose until death comes and then everything humanly is lost. Long before this happens, though, the individual living on the human level of consciousness has lost his faith, inner peace, confidence, joy of living, and happiness.

However, with the consciousness of the inner Presence of God, even to a very small degree, the individual makes great progress. Just think, your life today and every part of it can be increased 100 percent. And when you have let God increase it that much it can be increased another 100 percent. This increase can continue on infinitely as we increase our awareness of the inner Presence of God. There are no limitations to the expansion of God-consciousness.

How can this be done? Humanly we would like this increase to take place immediately. However we are usually not prepared for this great expansion of consciousness. We are usually reluctant to let go of our present beliefs and we are reluctant to do confidently what God reveals to us to do.

The development of the awareness of God is not done through human effort. High moral and ethical conduct does not develop this consciousness. But when the awareness comes and the consciousness is developed, one will be transformed and will live on an even higher level of moral and ethical behavior. Performing rituals and professing loyalty to an organization doesn't develop the consciousness, either, though when one is transformed he may express a loyalty and support comparable to his awareness. We cannot develop this consciousness through the mental method, which tells us to think of what we want to have or be and we will get it. This may work for getting a few outer things but not for getting the inner consciousness of the Presence of God. We cannot think our way into the kingdom of God.

God consciousness comes without human effort. In

fact, the more we can let go of human thought, emotion, and struggle after outer things, and really seek God with an open mind, the more this awareness will develop.

The method, if there is such, for developing this consciousness, is to study, meditate, and practice. Study truth, think about it and seek to discipline the mind and your actions. This is a preparation. Meditate daily, not only once but several or many times. Short periods to begin with; longer periods as you are led. "Be still and know that I am God." Always go to God in meditation with a completely open mind. This means no requests, no giving God deadlines to accomplish something for you. It also means a willingness to release whatever you have thought important and necessary for your life. Then begin to practice the higher consciousness. Do what your indwelling Spirit guides you to do, no matter how simple or unimportant it may seem to be. Increasing the first two without this third step will leave one on a plateau; little growth or development of consciousness will take place. Forget about the human anxiety and the fabulous promises and expectations given by those working on the mental level. Those expectations are not good enough for the wonders and blessings that will be bestowed upon you and through you from within. Forget about time. When the consciousness is developed the results will take place. Remember, "To them that hath it shall be given." Seeking to demonstrate and manifest things without the consciousness of the inner Presence of God is a waste of time. Unfortunately many are wasting much time, effort and money pursuing the empty promises of those working on the mental level.

There is One within you that Loves you and He will make His Presence known to you. You may know Him to a degree already. If you will only practice being still and letting go, He will come unto you and reveal more of Himself to you. And what a joy it will be! "To know thee is life eternal."

PRAYER AND MEDITATION

The most important thing we must learn to do in life is to pray and meditate. These are often relegated to emergency situations, a last ditch effort to survive some crisis, whereas they should be first. The practice of daily meditation and prayer will help us avoid the "end of the rope" situations and the feelings of despair and discouragement experienced by those who do not know their oneness with God. Most people do not know what prayer or meditation is, even though they may be doing something that they call prayer. Begging, beseeching, or pleading to an elusive God is not prayer. Thinking about making demonstrations of things, no matter how worthy and desirable and good, is not prayer.

True prayer is conscious communion with God. It is something that is real. It is a firsthand experience of realization of oneness with the presence of God within us. In this communion process we listen rather than talk; we receive advice rather than give it. In a time of quiet meditation when we are contemplating our relationship with God and realizing that He is the Source of all that we will ever need, the soul is uplifted and we do receive our help, our inspiration. We receive help even if a miracle demonstration does not take place immediately in our lives. As we grow in spiritual understanding we come to understand that the realization of God's presence within us precedes all manifestations and all development of consciousness. In true meditation we are willing to let consciousness grow in us.

This state of inner communion with God is called the Silence. In this state of receptivity all volitional thinking ceases. We do not think about problems and we do not even think about things that are desirable. A new type of communion is experienced. It is called realization or intuitive thinking. This is the process of letting God think through us, of letting God express through us. In these moments of inner communication more things are going on in consciousness than the human mind can perceive.

When one truly practices daily meditation and prayer he is gradually transformed. Paul called this process "dying daily." The human is elevated to the divine. The refining process of spiritual development is taking place, and slowly but surely the individual is transformed into a new person, a person that is more responsive to spiritual law than to human law, more responsive to God within his consciousness than to the human opinion of those around him.

The human part of us may fight to preserve its domain in consciousness. The old beliefs, attitudes, and traditions do not give up easily. In human thought and experience we often seek the company of those who comfort us in our limitations, those who counsel us that we are right and that if we persist, God will eventually change and grant our request. This is a waste of time and effort and energy for God will never change. There is no reason for God to change. It is we who must change so that God can express Himself, His good, through us.

As we persist in daily meditation and prayer the human ego will eventually die. All its attachments are eventually severed. All thought that our good comes from people or things outside of us is given up. This is when the soul truly becomes free, when the individual discovers and experiences true peace. This doesn't mean the individual dies physically. Nor does it mean there are no human relations. It simply means that on the spiritual level the individual isn't disturbed about not getting things from people and life, whereas on the human level, he would be disturbed.

Learning to pray is not easy. There are no quick or easy three-, four- or seven-step formulas to prayer even though many plans and formulas are offered. One must have a tailor-made experience and it must be developed by the individual. To learn to truly meditate and pray will take time, much time. It will take patience and persistent, consistent effort. It will take study. Some find it difficult to control their thinking when they try to meditate. It may be they need some intellectual training through the study of truth principles so they will know how to deal with some of the objections raised by human thought.

Meditation and prayer must be introduced into our daily schedule. Everything else must be secondary. Meditation time, prayer time must have first priority. This time of being alone with God in consciousness comes before family, friends, and all human experiences. We must have the determination that there will be no excuses, no rationalizations and no promises of make-up sessions the next day. It must be a seven day a week commitment. After all we eat at least three times a day with regularity and our times of prayer are more important than our times of eating. In fact the day will come when the sincere individual will spend more time in meditation than he will in eating food. When we learn to feed the soul properly we won't have so many physical cravings pestering us.

Why should we pray or meditate? The only reason and the only desire should be to know God. Jesus prayed for us to have this consciousness of oneness. His Prayer is recorded in the Gospel of John, the seventeenth chapter. In this prayer He says that to know God is to have eternal life. It is really to live. It will be a struggle for the human part of us to give up seeking God for things and experiences but this we must do. Every desire for some "thing" must be sacrificed for the desire to know God firsthand. The great prophet Jeremiah was a channel for God to speak these words of encouragement to us: "You shall seek me and find me when you shall search for me with all your heart." (Jer. 29:13)

The human part of us may question, "Is it really possible to know God?" The answer is a definite yes. The Psalmist, being a channel for the voice of God, says, "Be still and know that I am God." (Ps. 46:10) The human desire to get ahead, to get money, to have success, to achieve goals, to have or demonstrate physical health, must be given up. This doesn't mean they are not important or that we won't have them. It simply means we will not seek them, we will seek God. We remember Jesus said that these things will be added. Health will be added. Supply will be provided. Right relationships will be established. It will actually be a relief to the human to give up these desires.

We must make the decision to commit a definite time and a definite amount of time to prayer and to spiritual study. In the beginning this time should be well distributed throughout the day and night. This is an important commitment; it is a life-long commitment. We should begin with small increments of time in meditation. In the beginning, as with physical exercise, we should take it easy. The amount of time will increase as we go along.

The individual will discover wonderful things happening. His interests will change along with his physical tastes. The joy of prayer will soon supersede the joy of human and physical stimulation. When the mind is stimulated by true Reality, superficial human experiences will seem as nothing.

Meditation and prayer times should begin with the reading of some good truth literature from the Bible or some other source. I would suggest leaving aside the books that tell you how to get things. You want to go beyond this in order to have a true prayer experience. You can't use God to fulfill personal demands. You won't have to learn how to get anything. Our great challenge in life is to learn how to give. As you read you will find some statement that stands out. It may challenge your thought. It may even be shocking, but don't cast it out. Stop and enter your time of contemplative meditation. Dwell on the statement. Ask for illumination. Affirm, "Let there be light." Don't try to figure it out and don't be disturbed by its challenging content. Let the Spirit in you reveal to you the truth.

When this phase is mastered you will begin remaining quietly in meditation. In the beginning it may be only a few minutes but this will increase to as much as an hour or more. When you feel the release experience you will know that your soul has been filled. You will know the peace that passes all human understanding. The God you seek is within you. He is waiting for you. When the conditions of consciousness are right, His presence will be made known to you consciously and the joy of Jesus Christ will be made full in you.

SPIRITUAL HEALING

Unity is essentially a healing ministry. It began with the healing in the 1880s of Myrtle Fillmore, who had tuberculosis and had been given about six months to live. A friend suggested to her that she go hear a lecturer who was to speak one night in Kansas City. He was a metaphysical lecturer from Chicago and would be speaking on healing and other metaphysical teachings. What she heard that night began a healing process in her that was to change not only her life but the lives of many others in the years to come.

Myrtle believed that she had inherited her tuberculosis from her parents. It must have been quite startling to her when she heard the lecturer say, "You are a child of God; you do not inherit sickness." This was a totally new idea to her. It captured her thinking and she left that meeting with new hope and expectancy. Myrtle wasn't healed instantly, but she began improving and after seveal months she was totally healed of the tuberculosis. She was thirty-five when this healing took place and she lived to be eighty-six.

Tuberculosis was considered a serious illness in those days. People began hearing about her healing and they came to her for help. It was not a "laying on of hands" type of healing. This was something new. She began teaching these people a startling new idea about God within that can heal all conditions. It was healing through the transformation of consciousness. This transformation of consciousness was accomplished through the changing of the mind through teaching and prayer. Many people began experiencing healings. Myrtle's husband, Charles, became interested and even he was eventually healed of a serious ailment.

Healing takes place in three basic ways. First is the way of science. Medical science has done an outstanding work in helping people maintain their health. However,there are still many conditions that are considered incurable at the present time, for science hasn't found a cure for every known illness. In many instances science has not even discovered the basic causes and therefore can only treat the condition.

The second method is the mental process which is popular in the metaphysical movement today. Here again, results have been obtained by this method, but they are not totally satisfying. Some ailments have responded but there have been many that have not. This is also a very difficult method, for the ill person feels he must "work" at demonstrating health by repeating affirmations mentally, hoping to change beliefs in his subconscious mind, or he may feel that visualizing himself as being healed will bring forth the healing. Results may or may not be lasting through this method.

The third method, which is the method taught by Unity, is spiritual healing. This method seeks to heal the consciousness of the individual. It is the healing of the belief in separation from God. God is life, perfect life, and that life is within us right now. God's life within is fully capable of renewing and healing the physical body of any condition, and I stress, *any* condition. With God there are no incurable conditions.

We have within us all the ingredients necessary to express and manifest health in the body. But because of our lack of understanding we do not know how to express these ingredients so that we have this perfect health. We have many misconceptions about life. On the human level we think that life deteriorates as time goes by and yet it remains as pure and perfect as it ever was. This degeneration is even thought to be "natural." There is nothing natural about any illness. The natural thing is to have good health. The body is a self-renewing organism and would renew itself if there were no interference in consciousness.

The belief in separation from God, the Source of life and health, causes us much physical suffering and pain. It is also the cause of many other unpleasant things we experience. That is why many areas of our lives improve when we improve physically through the healing of consciousness.

Spiritual healing is simply getting back in tune with God. The body is a vehicle to express God-life. Imperfections in the body temple are not due to God but to our lack of understanding about life. God's perfect life within us is perfect now; it is not evolving into or becoming perfect, it already is perfect. This life is not affected by germs. Germs can only find habitation in the body when the consciousness is in need of healing of misconceptions about the self, God, and life.

When there is a need for spiritual healing the individual usually wants immediate, miraculous results. Spiritual healing can happen instantly if there is a change in consciousness, but it usually doesn't. So we must be patient with ourselves as we seek to grow in consciousness.

If we want a spiritual healing we must forget the condition and concentrate our effort on seeking the Cause of healing, God. We must concentrate on establishing the true healing connection in consciousness, oneness with God, oneness with life. Forgetting the condition means we cease thinking about the condition, we cease studying it and analyzing it and talking about it. This is especially true when we seek to pray. We do not have to tell God what is wrong. We do not have to give him a medical diagnosis. We do not have to figure out how the healing can or will take place. Our part is to come to a realization of faith that it can take place. The creative intelligence knows how to do what needs to be done. We don't even have to try mentally to help the healing process. In fact, mental effort can often interfere. We can't make healings happen; we can only let them happen.

Consciousness is healed through prayer. A realization of God's presence within us, which includes the feeling of oneness, comes to the individual who seeks God in daily meditation. We must be willing to become still and let go of all mental effort. Affirmations of health have their place and are for the purpose of helping to train the intellect in positive thinking about life. But the time comes when we must cease all this mental activity and learn to be still and receptive. Whenever we feel apprehensive about a physical need it is because we have been thinking about it too much, especially in a human, limited way. It is then that we must let go and be still and turn to God. God is something real within us and when the contact is made in consciousness we feel the release, peace, and assurance that healing is taking place.

In helping others it is important that we rise in consciousness and know the truth instead of dwelling on the other person's condition. We must forget the person and dwell on God and life. This is not lack of interest in the person, but a realization that the moment we get on the level of the personal we are on the level of limitation. The influence of a healing consciousness is omnipresent, for there is no space or time that has to be overcome. When a person needing help is open and receptive that person can be helped, can be healed. Maintaining a high level of consciousness would be very difficult to do while feeling sorry for someone or feeling discouraged because the condition has been classified as serious or incurable. That type of thinking must cease so that we can dwell in the consciousness of the presence of God.

If you want to develop a spiritual healing consciousness, sit as often as you can in quiet meditation. Do this, even if it seems nothing is happening in the outer. Remember the first effects of healing are inner effects, in consciousness, in the way we feel, and in the restoration of hope; then follow faith and assurance and peace of mind about the need for healing. As the consciousness is healing in this manner the physical body will be renewed and it will be renewed without mental effort. You will be marvelously surprised and amazed at what will happen in you and through you to help others.

PROSPERITY AND TRUE SUCCESS

When Jesus multiplied the bread and the fish He attracted a large following. But when He gave them the truth teaching, saying, "I am the bread of life" or "Eat my body and drink my blood" He lost most of them. These were hard sayings to the unillumined mind that was looking for the easy pickings of worldly goods.

The idea that we can be prospered is appealing and popular today. Many want to know how they can have more and how they can achieve more. Not only do they want more material goods to make them feel secure but they want the world's recognition to make them feel successful.

When a person comes across the positive thinking philosophy of truth, he not only asks the question, "Is it possible for me to have more?" but also "Is there enough to go around for everyone?" Well, the answer is "yes" to both questions. However, when one is truly prosperous and successful he doesn't make the seeking of money or things the total object of his existence. He discovers that the manifestation of things, including money, is the by-product of living the spiritual life, a life of service. He also discovers that the things are added easily without a lot of personal self-seeking.

The first step we must take toward true prosperity and success is an inner mental step. It is the inner recognition that God is the Source of all our good. God is the Source of all that we will ever have or express. God is the fulfillment. To get things without knowing God is not true success and whatever is achieved without God is meaningless and empty. There will be no secure feeling and there will no doubt be a nagging fear of losing the possessions. However, with God there is assurance that we will always be provided for. With God there is supply even in the so-called "hard times" we are supposed to be experiencing today.

The next step is to ask and answer, sincerely, this question, "Am I willing to do what is necessary to become really prosperous and to feel successful?" Note that the question states what is necessary, not what I superficially think is necessary, not what I would like to think is necessary or hope is necessary, but what is actually necessary, no matter how challenging it may seem to be.

A person may read about the visualization technique and be willing to spend much time reading about it and actually practicing it. He may even make quite an impressive list of things he wants to get, displaying them visually with pictures to help him in the visualization process. This technique will work. I know, for I have worked it. It was not totally satisfactory, however, and I have found far greater things have come forth without it. In fact the best things that have ever happened in my life happened without this mental effort. When the amount of time spent doing this is considered, including the length of time in days, weeks, months, and maybe years, and compared with the results obtained, it will be found that the results are meager at most.

Another method an individual may find that he is willing to spend time with is the repeated saying of affirmations. The true purpose of saying affirmations in this way is to gain realization and not to get things, but the neophyte doesn't understand this and he thinks that the mere repeating of affirmations will make him rich or help him achieve success. When these things do not happen he thinks there is nothing to this affirmation business and casts it aside as a waste of time and effort. When properly used to gain inner realization, the saying of affirmations and the contemplation of statements of truth are very helpful and when the realization is gained, then the outer manifestations of supply will come forth as needed.

Jesus was the greatest teacher of prosperity that ever appeared on the human scene. He promised great things if one would follow Him, keep His word, do the things He did, look to the Father, and believe that all things are possible. The great secret to a lasting prosperity and true success is contained in the statement He made which is, "GIVE AND IT SHALL BE GIVEN UNTO YOU, GOOD MEASURE, PRESSED DOWN, SHAKEN TOGETHER, AND RUNNING OVER SHALL MEN GIVE UNTO YOU."

When we go to God with a loaded "getting list" we are not receptive to finding out what we should give and how to give it. A person may say, "I will gladly give when I get something to give," but it doesn't work that way. Everyone has something he can begin giving right now, both materially and in the way of physical effort. Or he can even give in consciousness, such as prayer or thoughts and feelings of love. When a person thinks, "I will love him when he or she loves me" he is seeking to get before giving. However, if we are to work with spiritual principle we must seek to give, we must concentrate our thought on how we can give more of our money, time, talent, and ability in the services of humanity. We don't do this the way humanity may think we should, but the way God guides us.

Now I will tell you another way the great prosperity secret is expressed in the Bible. Abraham knew the secret, followed it and was a multimillionaire. Jacob knew it and did it and was similarly blessed. There were many others who knew the secret and were blessed accordingly, some with material wealth and others in various other ways. All were prospered in that their needs were always provided for; and all were truly successful, for they were doing what

God guided them to do. The secret is contained in this statement which is given in the form of a promise. It is, "BRING YE ALL THE TITHES INTO THE STORE-HOUSE AND PROVE ME NOW HEREWITH, SAITH THE LORD OF HOSTS, IF I WILL NOT OPEN THE WINDOWS OF HEAVEN AND POUR YOU OUT A BLESSING THAT THERE SHALL NOT BE ROOM ENOUGH TO RECEIVE IT."

This is one of the greatest secrets of prosperity and even when a person knows about it on the human level he fails to recognize it as a prosperity principle. The human mind thinks of it as a sure way to go broke. But the tithe commitment is the entering into a working agreement and relationship with God. Instead of working just for self we work with God to "feed his sheep," or as it is also stated, "to feed the poor." This is not an easy commitment to make, but it is one that leads to great spiritual growth.

What is tithing? It is the commitment to give to God one tenth of our gross monetary income from all channels. It is putting our supply in circulation to "feed his sheep," or again, to "feed the poor." And who are the poor? They are the millions who do not know the truth about the kingdom of God within them. This includes many outwardly rich people. There are poor poor people and poor rich people. Jesus said that His message, His "good news" about the kingdom should be preached around the world. He also stated that the harvest is plenty, meaning there are many who are seeking, but the laborers are few, meaning there are few willing to make the commitment that is really necessary to get the word of truth around the world.

Many people are spiritually starving to death. If they were richly fed the truth, they would or could begin to live. Many times we get really concerned about feeding the body, but it is the soul that needs to be fed.

A person doesn't tithe just to get more money. A person tithes to get free of the hold money has on him. He tithes to become a free and open channel to work with God in feeding the sheep the truth. The commitment to tithe, to take God as a financial partner, usually comes early in the student's search for truth. However, the magnitude of the challenge often causes the student to put it aside for future implementation when things are better or when he is better able to do it. Little does he realize that it is the implementation of this commitment that leads to the very things he would like to have—financial security, health, happiness, true success.

Where should we give our tithe? When the commitment is made to God, we can be sure we will be shown. We will be shown that giving to relatives is not tithing. We will be shown that giving to the highest and best spiritual teaching, usually the very one we are involved in, is where we will be led to give so that that teaching may be given more fully and freely.

THE DEVELOPMENT OF FAITH

After Jesus' transfiguration experience He came down from the mountain with Peter and John and returned to the other disciples. They had been asked by a man to heal his son of epilepsy but they were not having any success. When the boy's father saw Jesus he ran to Him and asked Jesus to heal the boy. Jesus said, "O faithless and perverse generation, how long shall I be with you? How long shall I suffer you? Bring him hither to me." (Mat. 17:17) They brought the boy to Jesus and Jesus healed him instantly.

Later the disciples asked Jesus why they could not heal the boy. Jesus said, "Because of your little faith: for verily I say unto you, if ye have faith as a grain of mustard seed, ye shall say unto this mountain, 'Remove hence to yonder place,' and it shall remove; and nothing shall be impossible unto you." (Mat. 17:20)

The development of and outstanding use of faith was a major emphasis in the teaching of Jesus. He stated that it was possible for us to have such great faith that not only would we all be able to heal but we would also be able to do the things that He did and even greater things. Evidently we are living on less than a mustard seed amount of faith. And yet some pretty wonderful things are accomplished in our lives.

The word faith is used in a number of ways. Some use it to mean a religious affiliation or the acceptance of some theological precepts. Faith as Jesus taught it is certainly more than the acceptance of religious creeds. That would hardly move a molehill, much less a mountain.

On one occasion as Jesus was walking down the road a

woman came up behind Him and touched the hem of His garment. She had been thinking to herself that she might be healed if she could only touch the hem of His garment. She was healed and Jesus, realizing that something had happened, turned around, saw the woman, and said to her, "Thy faith has made thee whole." (Mat. 9:22)

Later when two blind men asked Jesus to heal them, Jesus first asked them, "Believe ye that I am able to do this?" They said they believed. Jesus then touched their eyes and said, "According to your faith be it unto you." (Mat. 9:29)

What is this fantastic quality we call faith? The writer of Hebrews tell us, "Now faith is the assurance of things hoped for, a conviction of things not seen." (Heb. 11:1) Coming alive with faith is something that happens in a person, inspiring that individual with assurance and a conviction even though there may be no outer reason for believing that anything good can happen. In fact a person's situation may seem totally hopeless and still that feeling of assurance can be very strong.

We might say that faith is an inner perception of some impending good. It is a non-intellectual perception and therefore not based on logic and reason. We can't think our way into a faith consciousness by thinking; it just happens when the consciousness is properly prepared. Faith may even be considered therefore an inner knowing and this knowing may contradict our human reasons and expectations as to what is and what is not possible. A person with this dynamic experience of faith can face and stand firm in assurance even in the most negative of situations. One without this faith usually experiences hopelessness and despair.

In a consciousness of faith we see this world through opened eyes. We see it, not as a physical world but as a spiritual world, a world not subject to human laws of limitation but subject only to spiritual laws that are eternal and unlimited. Faith widens our perspective of life and we behold infinite possibilites of good, not only for ourself but for everyone. Yet we know these things cannot be done through personal effort alone for we cannot make ourselves believe. Faith isn't developed through the repeating of affirmations, no matter how strongly we affirm that we believe.

How is this great faith developed? First, we must realize, in a positive and realistic but not limiting way, that it will not be easy to develop the faith that Jesus talked about. There may be many frustrating moments as we make the attempt to do what is necessary. There may even be crying periods and expressions of anger. There will definitely be sacrifices that will have to be made. Not only will many of our treasured beliefs have to be given up but we may even be required to give up some of our associations, especially those of a dependent nature. Much of this will be a soul-purifying preparation for the receiving of this free gift of faith from God. The woman who was healed by the touch of his garment had been searching, expecting, and trying for twelve years. What seemed like an instantaneous miracle therefore turns out to be a twelve-year miracle. The man healed at the pool of Bethsaida had been living and hoping for thirty-eight years. So his was an instantaneous thirty-eight year miracle.

For some there may be shorter times. It depends upon the individual and how open and receptive that person may really be. Most of us haven't reached the point in consciousness where we have been willing to sacrifice to the extent necessary for a genuine faith experience. We have so focused on wanting things to excite and stimulate us physically and have concentrated our energies of mind and soul upon getting these things. But this outer seeking and the mental effort of trying to get things has been detrimental to developing inner receptivity.

Paul tells us simply how faith is developed. In one way it is simple and seems so easy. But until we break through the human resistance in consciousness, the development of faith will be very difficult. I am emphasizing the challenge, not to discourage, but to remove any illusions we may have about it. Now, Paul said, "Faith cometh by hearing, and hearing by the word of God." (Rom. 10:17) The word of God is the Presence of God within you, me, and everyone. It is the same God that was in Jesus. Jesus listened to that God within Him and God was able to do marvelous things through Him. We are attuned to the outer world of limitation. We therefore must discipline ourselves so that we can practice the art of listening to the inner guidance. We must eventually do this all the time, morning, noon, and night, and all the time in between. You will remember Jesus said, "Watch and pray for you know not the hour when your Lord cometh." You cannot know when you will be ready in consciousness for the coming realization of the inner presence and the receiving of the free gift of faith.

We must be patient and not anxious about getting ahead or getting something; we must keep listening and keep expecting. Although we as humans can hear audible sounds we are in many respects totally deaf to the spiritual vibes of God within us. The "still small voice" seems so still and so small and yet when the inner ear is opened and we hear the voice of Spirit, it will seem quite loud. It will be unmistakable. It will be very practical even though to some in human limited thought it may seem very impractical. It will have a silencing effect upon us. We will realize that we do not have to save our family or the world; that we do not have to run around telling all the non-believers and trying to get them to believe.

In that moment of conscious contact with the indwelling spirit of God we will receive the gift of faith to the degree that we are prepared. It may be less than a mustard seed amount, but remember that can do fantastic things. We will realize that the receiving of this free gift of faith is dependent on what we do outwardly but only to the degree of inner receptivity. We don't have to be pure and perfect to receive it. How can we be pure and perfect without faith?

When it comes, then we will be able to speak the word of truth with authority and it will move not only us but all things in our world that need moving. You will ask whatsoever you will and it shall be done. Of course with this faith there will certainly be the wisdom to ask only for those things that are for our highest good. The thrill, joy, inner security and assurance are well worth the time and effort we put into the inner seeking of a conscious realization of God.

"I AND MY FATHER ARE ONE"

When Jesus made the statement, "I and my Father are one," the people listening to Him wanted to stone Him. To them it was blasphemy to put the human self on the same level with God. They said, "Being a man you make yourself a God." Today, after almost 2,000 years of theological training most of us have no difficulty accepting Jesus as a son of God, but to these people He was just another human being, the son of Joseph and Mary, a carpenter's son.

Jesus reminded them of the words of the Psalmist, "I say, 'You are gods, sons of the Most High, all of you.'" (Psalms 82:6) He was saying that not only was He the son of God but that everyone was the son of God. The words are true today even though we haven't fully realized their meaning. Intellectually you are being told one of the great secrets of life, a truth that most people are not aware of.

Right this moment you are one with God. You always have been one with God and you will always be one with Him. This is true whether you believe it or not; whether you know it or not; whether you understand it or not. Wherever you go throughout life, you will always be one with God, whether in the body or out of the body. When you feel alone God is with you. In your moments of joy He is there. There cannot be any separation whatsoever and if you can accept it there cannot even be any distinction between you and God in Reality.

Now we may think that we are separated from God due to our thinking based upon the outer world of appearances. We may have accepted what we have been told, that

God is up in the sky or somewhere else, and because of this type of thinking we may even feel we are separated from God. But these are illusions; we are always one with God in spite of them.

One of our great objects in life should be to gain a conscious realization of oneness with God. We must gain this awareness to the same degree that we are aware of the physical world in which we live. We must rise above all sense of separation and seek the Presence until we discover it. Nothing in life will ever satisfy us. Soul restlessness will never cease until we know and feel our oneness with God.

You may search high and low for some "thing," thinking it will make you happy or make you feel important and successful. Or you may seek some relationship, thinking that some person can make you happy. But though you gain everything physical, though you experience everything possible, though you go everywhere on the face of this earth and a few places beyond it, none of these will quench the thirst of the soul to know God.

Some people are hoping to find and see God after they die. They are only delaying the time right now when they can know God and feel His Presence within them. These people are "wanderers in the wilderness" of materiality. To them life is a struggle and a hardship, something to get out of as soon as possible. Many are like those who listened to Jesus, they hear the truth and can't accept it even though it is what they thought they were expecting. The people listening to Jesus asked Him to tell them plainly if He were the Christ, the Messiah. He told them their problem was that they could not believe, for He had told them many times that He was the Christ, and He had done some marvelous works.

I would venture to say that if He appeared today in the flesh in this world many who professed to believe in Him would be just as doubtful. They would want some proof, especially if He did not come the way they were expecting

Him to come. Many people are living with a dream they don't expect to come true. They don't expect to see Jesus really, and they don't expect to see God or know God. How empty they must feel, thinking, believing, and feeling that way.

There are some who have caught a glimpse of the inner light. They know their oneness with God although not as fully as Jesus did. Jesus would say to those today as He did to some years ago, "You are not far from the kingdom." These individuals have a feeling or sense of a Presence in their lives. Even though they have great challenges, the Presence is there. It never leaves them. Even if they make mistakes, serious mistakes, the Presence is there. Our friends or relatives may desert us or reject us because of our mistakes, but not the Presence, not God.

This consciousness of the Presence of God saves us and helps us, and provides for our every need. Even when there is no visible evidence of help, God's help is there and His help is never limited. If we would learn to trust the Presence more, greater things would happen in our lives. But the sensory world seems more reliable and dependable, yet it is so limiting and disappointing. When we depend on God instead of people we will never be disappointed. God can do for us what people can't do. People have their human limitations and no matter how wonderful they are or how much they can do for us, they can never totally satisfy the need of our soul to know God.

Even a small degree of realization of oneness with God will satisfy our human desires and cravings. With God they will either be fulfilled or dissolved. An interesting thing happens as we discover more and more our oneness with God; we find we don't really want or need all we think we need. The things we thought we couldn't live without are in many instances no longer desirable or even needed. This doesn't mean that the elimination of relationships and things will make us feel any more one with

God. But as we grow and become more aware of God and feel His Presence in our lives each day, we will be less dependent upon the material world for soul support, for happiness, for joy, for meaning and for purpose.

The soul's hunger and thirst for God can never be quenched through physical stimulation or indulgence. Eating food will not do it. Sex will not do it. Drinking will not do it. Drugs will not do it. No form of physical stimulation will do it even if it seems harmless. These things only pacify for a time. The unfortunate thing is that they must eventually be increased in order to produce the same physical pleasure as before, and this increase may be the very thing that will eventually destroy the individual.

Conscious oneness with God eliminates the need for self-seeking with all its hazards and disappointments. When we find God we realize our importance to Him, to ourselves and to life. We don't have to get others to think we are important; they may never think that way. When we abide in the consciousness of His Presence we find joy, happiness, and fulfillment in doing even the simple things we are called upon to do. We find that we do not have to make a name for ourselves, for that ceases to be important. We don't have to gain worldly recognition. We don't have to leave our footprints in this world.

When we look to God He speaks to us as He did through Jesus and says to us, "Come unto me all ye who are weary and heavy-laden and I will give you rest unto your souls." And what a rest and relief it is! We are free of the need to struggle, to fight, to manipulate. We find that we don't have to be on top of the heap in human terms to be a success. There are many life failures who have humanly made it.

How can we gain or increase our awareness of oneness with God? A good way to begin is to take the statement Jesus made, "I and my Father are one," and contemplate its true meaning. Think about it, ask questions of the

Father about it. Let it run through your mind many times throughout the day. Begin your day thinking about your oneness with God. Know that He is guiding you in everything you do each day. The secret: the more you can release your human desires and dependencies and relax your human strivings, the sooner the realization will come or the greater the expansion of awareness will be.

Intensify your longing to know and experience God. We are told, "You shall seek me and find me when you search for me with all your heart." Remember, God wants to be found; He wants to make His Presence felt in your mind and heart. He wants to uplift you and encourage you so that you always feel His great love for you.

HOW TO MEET OBSTACLES

"WHEN THE GOING GETS TOUGH, THE TOUGH GET GOING." This popular quote is used to encourage us to keep on pushing and trying and putting forth even greater effort when we are confronted with obstacles to our goals. There is a degree of truth in the statement but there is another side that we should consider.

For example, if we are on the wrong path to our good and we keep on trying, we are only wasting our time and causing ourselves undue anxiety and frustration. If we meet and overcome one obstacle we will only find another one waiting for us. We can use will-power to find our way along the personal path we have chosen to follow, but if that path is out of harmony with the better, divine way, we are creating our own obstacles.

We can achieve a degree of success. We may become rich; we may even get recognition that makes us famous; we may even get a healing, but we will have to support all this with will-power and constant vigilance. We will probably not be very happy or satisfied and will be looking for greater things to accomplish. There will be no true peace or feeling of worthwhile accomplishment.

The only way to have true and lasting prosperity, health, and happiness is to get in tune with God, Who is within us, and let Him guide us and direct us along the path that will lead to our greatest good. He knows us better than we know ourselves. He knows that many of our personal desires will not be satisfying and will only lead to misery and unhappiness. He will help us to avoid many unhappy experiences by leading us in a way that is truly satisfying.

When we are confronted with what seems to be an obstacle to some goal, even a goal we think is the right one, we need to let go. Instead of toughening up with personal determination we need to loosen up with spiritual resolve. Personal determination is the attitude that we are going to keep on trying and making the effort no matter what stands in the way. Spiritual resolve is the willingness to let go and let God take charge, the willingness to do what He leads us to do, even if it means giving up our personal plans and goals. So, we might rephrase the opening quote in this way, "WHEN THE GOING GETS TOUGH, THE SPIRITUALLY TOUGH LET GO." It does take spiritual strength to let go. After all we may have been dreaming our personal dream for a long time and we may feel a great deal of happiness depends upon its fulfillment.

However, what we really need is the realization that God is in charge. We need to let Him do the work of removing obstacles that may only seem to stand in the way. What we think may be an obstacle in our lives may only be a negative attitude in our own mind. For example, if we think that someone can keep our good from us or keep God's good plan for us from expressing and manifesting, that person is not the obstacle, our attitude is our only obstacle.

We may think that a healing need is an obstacle but it can actually be a blessing that will help us realize the need for letting go and letting God take charge of our lives, a time for reconsideration of our goals and aims in life to see if we are in tune with God or to see whether we are pursuing our personal ambitions.

So, as a first step in meeting what may seem to be an obstacle, I would strongly suggest that you let go and let God. Relax and let go of trying to figure out how you will conquer or get around what seems to be an obstacle to you. Seek only to get in tune with God's direction for you and let Him take care of the obstacle. This is not giving up in despair; it is letting go in faith.

The next step is much easier than all the personal striving and brings greater, inner peace. Stand still in faith and realize that there is a solution, there is an answer. No matter how great the obstacle, there is a way to meet it successfully. You may think there is no way out, but with God there is always a way.

At this time a person who does not have this faith in God may do something negative when he thinks there is no solution to his problem. He may even go so far as to commit suicide. Many are taking this route today. Others try to eliminate the obstacle or run from it. However, this is a good time to remind ourselves of the Bible passages that tell us to "Stand still and see the salvation of the Lord . . . the battle is not yours, but mine, saith the Lord." Quite often, more can be achieved in simply doing nothing, except trusting, than in putting forth much effort.

Developing this consciousness of trust so that we can stand firm in the realization that with God there is a solution comes through the regular practice of prayer and daily study of truth principles. In prayer times truth is revealed to us. We are shown the best way to meet what seem to be obstacles and if we take this advice from the Lord within us, we will be successful. In study the intellect and emotions are trained and disciplined and consciousness is developed so that we can accept and follow the light that shines within us.

If we have been faithful and persistent in prayer and study we will be able to let go and stand still with peace of mind. When there is a need for healing we will not have to wonder whether God wants us to be healed, we will know

He does. We won't get into the negative state of mind that accepts illness as God's way of punishing us or that thinks in terms of incurable diseases. Instead, we will know these things are false and can reject them and give our thought to the possibility and expectancy of healing.

The same applies to any area of life. God wants us to be happy, prosperous, and successful. Daily study will help us to train our thinking and feeling natures to be in harmony with this basic truth. It will also build a powerful consciousness that will sustain us when we are confronted with an obstacle and when we may be experiencing moments of wondering, questioning, searching, doubting, and even moments of discouragement. It is the unconscious development of God's Presence that we have established that works in our lives. We may call it the "grace of God," but the grace of God can work for us only when we have consciousness established.

We may not see how God can change events and people and we do not need to see how it is going to be done. There may be times when we are on the right path but need only to stand firm and trust until our consciousness is developed further. Some people get illumination about truth and the opportunities it offers and want to go out immediately and demonstrate it. They want to demonstrate prosperity without a prosperity consciousness. They think the superficial reading of a few books on prosperity will make them rich or that going to a pep rally type seminar on prosperity will do it. These things have their place and may aid in the development of consciousness. However, a true prosperity consciousness based on faith and trust in God isn't usually developed in one session. It is the result of persistent study and prayer.

So my third suggestion would be, "Be patient and grow." Develop your consciousness, a quality consciousness that really makes for peace and prosperity. Some work at this only when the obstacles arise. The wise person works at the continual development of consciousness during the periods of calm in his or her life.

Whatever looms before you that you think is an obstacle is an opportunity to prove that these three suggestions will work. Try them: Let go and let God. Stand still in faith realizing that there is a solution. Be patient with yourself and grow; develop the consciousness through which God can work to bless you.

THE VALUE OF FRIENDSHIP

Joseph Scriven, author of the well-known hymn, "What a Friend We Have in Jesus," had a disappointing experience with his friends and discovered there is a difference between true friends and acquaintances. He mentions this disappointment in the last verse when he says, "Do thy friends despise, forsake thee." True friends do not, neither do they use us to achieve some personal gain on their part.

It is unfortunate that this same thing is going on in religion today on the campus of Colorado University. Seeking converts to Christianity some Christians are making friends with those whom they think are good prospects for salvation. This is easy to do since many of the young people in colleges probably are lonely and want friends. However, if they do not convert they are rejected eventually by those who tendered the gestures of friendship in the name of Jesus Christ. I don't believe Jesus would have approved of these techniques. He never rejected those who were considered publicans and sinners. In fact he made some statements that those who think they have it made should consider. Jesus said, "The sons of darkness will enter the kingdom before the sons of light."

Jesus was a friend of His disciples. Peter denied Him three times but they were still true friends. Judas betrayed Him but I'm sure the friendship tie remained.

One of the outstanding stories in the Bible on friendship is that of David and Jonathan. Jonathan was the eldest son of Saul, the first king of Israel. David was a soldier in Saul's army. He had come up through the ranks from a harp-playing lad, soothing the weary mind of Saul, to a highly successful soldier. In fact when the army returned from a victory the people would shout, "Saul has slain his thousands and David his ten thousands." This made Saul very jealous. In addition to this the prophet Samuel said that David would be the next king to replace Saul and this added fuel to the jealous spirit in Saul. Eventually Saul became enraged and decided to eliminate David.

Jonathan, being a good friend of David, kept David informed of his father's plans to kill him. One time Jonathan even rebuked his father and got his father to promise he would not kill David so that David could return to the city. Saul later broke his promise and David had to flee for his life. Eventually Saul and Jonathan were both killed in a battle. When David heard the news he wrote a poem honoring them, and gave instructions that the poem be learned by all the people. In the poem he says of Jonathan, "How are the mighty fallen in the midst of the battle! Jonathan lies slain upon thy high places. I am distressed for you my brother Jonathan; very pleasant have you been to me; your love to me was wonderful, passing the love of women."

Friendship is something to be cherished. A person without friends or a friend is an unfortunate and lonely person. I suppose if we were to take a poll of what people really want in life, we would probably find the desire for a true friend or friends to be near the top of the list of important desires. In many instances it would come before the desire for money.

Quite often a strong bond of friendship is cherished more than blood relationships, as in the case of Jonathan and David. Jonathan loved his father Saul and respected him, but he couldn't go along with his father in his attempt to kill David. He loved David and protected and helped him. Jonathan also gave up his right to the throne, for he recognized the superiority of David. After all,

David had accepted the challenge of the giant Goliath while all the other Hebrew soldiers, including Jonathan, were fearful of the giant.

A friend is one with whom we share mutual interests, one who accepts us as we are with all our limitations and still appreciates our companionship. A true friend doesn't try to make us into a new person through critical suggestions. A friend is one whose approval, acceptance and praise helps to draw out of us confidence, a feeling of self-worth and other good qualities. Quite often a person feels better and is happier with a friend than he is with a relative.

True friendship is an important ingredient in an enduring marriage relationship. Unfortunately many marriages never get a chance for this advanced development. A marriage which is not based on the true bond of friendship will become rocky when the fires of romantic love cool. Without friendship the individuals begin complaining about each other's shortcomings instead of enjoying each other's attributes. If there are no mutual interests beyond the initial passions there isn't much hope of developing a true friendship. But in a relationship made in heaven—that is, one established in love—friendship in marriage can develop and the relationship becomes enduring and even more meaningful. This happens in a true friendship for each one seeks to give more to the relationship than he or she gets out of it. And that is what a true friendship is all about. It is not the seeking of advantages, benefits, or favors; it is the seeking to give and to share.

In giving and sharing we also discover that we find inner peace, joy, happiness, security, and freedom; the relationship is not one where we feel in bondage.

A friend is a priceless gem that can't be purchased and it is a gem that increases in value as the years go by. We should do all we can to protect the friendship, never making our friends a scapegoat for our negative thoughts and emotions. We must show respect for another's opinions and ideas for one's ideas are precious and important. We must respect them even if we disagree with them. We must emphasize our points of agreement and put the others aside. If a friend happens to have a problem, challenge, or life situation that seems to us as an evil, we should seek to understand instead of being critical or instead of terminating the relationship. If we make perfection in moral habits the basis for friendship we may never have any friends, for after all none of us is perfect. It may be that a helping hand will some day be needed by our friend to help him in overcoming some undesirable habit or practice.

There is one true friend that we all have and that is God within us, the inner friend. He is always there to offer love and appreciation and to point out our potential. He never condemns us for our mistakes. He never rejects us. His love is so great and unconditional that we find it difficult to comprehend and even accept. With this friend we will never feel lonely. Many people go to parties and other places where there are crowds and still feel lonely. They may even be with a small, select group of human friends and still feel lonely. However, when a true relationship is established with the inner friend we never feel that way and this makes it possible for us to enjoy our outer friends that much more.

In Proverbs 18:24 the writer tells us that if we are to attract and develop friendships we must first develop a friendly attitude. He states, "A man that hath friends must show himself friendly." Some show their hostility, but this only repels people. An optimistic attitude toward life makes for a pleasant consciousness and a radiant personality and this will attract friends. We like to be around people who are cheerful and pleasant, for they lift our spirit and this is a great need in the world today.

THE ORDERLY PROCEDURE

Many new buildings are rising on the downtown Denver skyline, buildings of all sizes, heights, shapes, colors, and appearance. Some might be called beautiful; some might be called ghastly. However, regardless of all these differences, there is something that they all have in common. They have all been built on the same basic engineering principles. A hole was dug in the ground, a foundation was laid, the steel superstructure installed, and so on from the ground up. None was started from the top down. There was an orderly procedure in bringing forth the finished structure. By following the basic principles the result was a building standing on a firm foundation.

A number of years ago we put a man on the moon. Scientists, in doing so, adhered to certain basic principles that had been discovered over a period of time. They were very meticulous in complying with those principles. They were more concerned with that than they were with the cost of complying. The scientists didn't make the principles, they only discovered them; they could not change any of them even if they had wanted to.

This brings us to a basic truth for living a good life and it is this: "EVERYTHING, INCLUDING ALL HUMAN BEINGS, IS GOVERNED BY UNIVERSAL, ETERNAL, AND UNCHANGING LAWS." We may have thought that the scientific principle, "for every action there is an opposite and equal reaction," applied only to inanimate objects, but it also applies to human beings. Since thought is an action, then for every thought there is some reaction even though it may be ever so small. We humans are a part of this universe. If we discover these laws and work with them, we can control our destiny instead of being subject to the physical elements.

Although there are many sizes and shapes of airplanes flying in the sky, they all do so because of the same principles. When a principle is violated, either through error, lack of awareness, or deliberate intent, the result is failure or tragedy. It makes no difference who is involved, what their religious beliefs may be, or what special favors they may think they have in their relationship with God. It makes no difference whether they are "good" according to cultural values or "bad." The important thing is how they relate to principles. As Jesus said, the rain falls on the just and the unjust. Of course, if one is unjust in principle, there will be a time of compensation.

For everything that you or I want to accomplish there are certain basic principles that must be adhered to for achievement. If I want to be prospered I must accept and apply the prosperity principles. If I want health, I must apply the laws for healthy living. These are not only physical, pertaining to what I eat and drink, but they are also mental, emotional, and spiritual.

We may have thought that we are the products of chance or the special manifestation of a capricious god. However, nothing in this universe happens by chance. We may not know why something happens and that is what we should admit, instead of attributing things to an unknown god or giving other reasons such as fate or chance. Before humans had a scientific knowledge of the universe they thought "spirits" were present in everything, causing them to move—trees moving, storms, rivers flowing. They even thought there were spirits in rocks. There is still much that we do not know about life and its many laws. In fact more is unknown than is known. It is this lack of knowing that causes many of our problems. Even when we know, we don't always do what we know we should do.

Knowing that our lives are determined by principle and how we relate to it is most encouraging. It is encouraging for it means that in principle there is a solution to every problem; there is a way to fulfill every good desire. If we take the time and make the effort to discover the necessary principles then, as Jesus said, anything is possible. So our problem is not to keep wondering whether we can be healed or prospered but to discover and apply the principles in an orderly way.

The orderly way is to follow the guidance of Spirit, God, within us. Using or attempting to use principle for personal gain is never satisfying even if we do get some astounding results. Take for example the principle of love. We all want to be loved and we all seek it because we think it will make us happy, give us peace or harmony. Now, many get love from others but they may not get the peace, happiness, and harmony. However, if they give love, true spiritual love, freely and unconditionally, they will always have peace, happiness, and harmony.

Another thing about the use of principle is this: a higher knowledge of life's principles enables one to do things that seem miraculous. The primitive human being, dwelling in a cave and rubbing two sticks together trying to get a fire started would be quite startled if a modern type human had come along with a match or cigarette lighter and started one.

Jesus had a higher knowledge of the laws of life and He was trying to teach them to us. We have thought that His seemingly miraculous actions were suspensions of the laws of life, but they were not. All things were done by principles we are not aware of but which can be discovered by anyone. Jesus knew this and that is why He stated that the works He did could be done by each and every one of us.

The rules or principles of life are always for our good. There is for example no principle of sickness or dying, but there is the great principle of life which will enable us to have perfect health.

Jesus and other great prophets and teachers have come to teach us the rules for successful living. They have not always been popular. They have been misunderstood because their ideas have been too idealistic. This was due to the ignorance of those who thought they would lose by the new knowledge, for new knowledge makes old methods and traditions obsolete.

Jeremiah was an Old Testament prophet who came along and tried to get the king and the people to follow the guidance of the Lord. However, they were too secure in their prosperity and they thought that since God was in their Temple nothing could happen to them. They were quite mistaken. There were many more popular prophets who were saying that things were fine and that the king and people should not listen to Jeremiah. The popular prophets were wrong and tragedy came.

A prophet is a teacher who truly understands principle and seeks to communicate it to others in order to help them. There are various grades of prophets or teachers. As in the days of Jeremiah we have today "popular prophets" who tell the people what they want to hear instead of what they need to hear regarding principle. Their messages sound something like a headline in a sensational newspaper which says, "How to eat or drink what you want and lose weight" or "How to get something for nothing" or "How to be successful without any effort on your part." They are like the piano salesman who says, "Buy my piano and I will teach you how to play overnight without any practice. You don't need any lessons; all you need to do is follow my special technique."

Many people are being deluded today in the metaphysical field by these same type prophets who offer health, prosperity, success, and fame without any "practice." Health, prosperity, and success are possible but they can only be established through the persistent application of principle and this will take much effort. We will have to practice. We will have to practice meditation. We will have to seek the guidance of the Lord within us. We will have to be willing to change our beliefs and attitudes. We will have to take time to study life's principles.

It is a human tendency to seek out those who make the easy promises and avoid those who make higher demands on us. But these latter are the ones we should really seek, for they can lead us to a greater understanding of principle that would give true mastery and dominion over our lives. Jesus made high demands on us. He knew we were capable of achieving great things in life. To have the knowledge and understanding of the rules is to be assured of health, prosperity, and many other blessings.

WHAT SHALL IT BE?

Every decision we make offers us the possibility of a positive or negative result. What shall it be is up to us.

A pessimist would no doubt see more obstacles and would let these guide him in making his decision. A self-disciplined optimist may see the same obstacles but he would also see possibilities of overcoming them or at least would believe that ways could be found to overcome them.

Your present and future happiness will be determined by your decisions. When pondering over what shall it be we should remember that the negative attitudes of the majority do not have to influence us. Consider some of the negative ways of thinking that paralyze many people.

When the obstacle or challenge seems really great the question arises, "Shall I mentally accept this limitation?" How many times have we accepted defeat simply because we assumed there was no way to solve the problem. After accepting defeat we then train ourselves to live with the limitation without any hope of ever changing it. This is supposed to be psychologically healthy—to find a degree of tranquility through acceptance of something about which it seems nothing can be done. If we accept some situation as being impossible then we will have to do this. But I doubt there will be any real tranquility and peace of mind, especially when Jesus states, "If you can believe, all things are possible."

Should some misfortune or tragedy happen we should not assume that it is the end of happiness as so many often do. What shall it be? Shall it be a life of misery, discouragement, despair, and unhappiness? Or shall it be a life of renewed expectations of good?

Some have accepted society's judgment that success and prosperity are difficult to achieve after a certain age. That age has been set as low as 40. Some people stay in an unhappy job situation simply because they feel no one will hire them after 40. Others raise the age to 50 or 65. Yet, the possibilities of success are unlimited at any age. What shall it be? Shall we accept society's judgment or shall we accept God's guidance, His ideas that would lead us to as great a success as we are willing to achieve?

What shall it be? Shall I let circumstances determine my goals in life? Some people decide this is the best thing to do. We should remember that God has given us the power and ability to change circumstances. We should set as goals those ideas that He reveals to us. Success comes only in following this inner guidance.

We are confronted each day with many decisions that will affect us. Our spiritual growth, which is most important, can be delayed. If one fails to pursue a study of truth after the experience of illumination or fails to practice daily prayer and meditation he is only delaying the spiritual and material blessings that could be his.

We have to make many decisions each day that will have a tremendous effect upon our health. Delay in making changes in destructive habits will delay the healing process.

What shall it be? It is up to us. We have to make the decisions; no one can do it for us even though we would like for them to. It may be challenging to make these decisions, but our good in the present and the future depends on making positive and constructive decisions.

Avoidance of making them will not make them turn out right. The "what is to be, will be" philosophy of life is totally false; things do not happen by fate or chance. This attitude reveals a shortsighted view of life. There is no predetermined destiny set by God. The only thing that might be considered as being predetermined is that one day every person will know and experience the power, mastery, and dominion of Jesus Christ. There is no uncertainty about life. We may not know why certain things happen but we can be sure they do not happen by chance. We as humans are ignorant of the many and complex causes that determine every event. We attribute causes to people, germs, and events when we know in truth that all causes originate in consciousness. We spend most of our time trying to control what we think are outer causes. If we would spend a portion of that time seeking to correct the causes in consciousness we would all be blessed to a greater degree.

Also, we are unaware of our potential power to influence causes and therefore make little effort to change a negative "what shall it be" to a positive one.

The spiritual potential within you is unlimited. It is the spiritual that will give you mastery of the material. Jesus suggested that we should seek this inner, spiritual potential. He called it the search for the kingdom of God. He said, "The kingdom of God is within you." Many people spend their lives searching around the world for fame and fortune and good health while all the time the Source and Cause of all these things is right within their own soul consciousness. Jesus said that if we would seek this kingdom and its righteousness, all the outer things would be added. The wonderful thing is that they will be added without the struggle, toil, and frustration we experience as a result of trying to get things in the human way. The most important lesson we can learn as we begin our journey along the spiritual path of light is the lesson of *letting* God work through us instead of trying to force Him to work through us. We must train ourselves to let Him express His ideas through us instead of formulating our plans as to what we think is best.

It will be challenging for the human part of us to let go, but if we can once convince ourselves of the utter futility of the human way and undertake the new way of letting, we will have done ourselves one of the greatest favors in life.

There is a story in the Bible about Adam naming the birds and beasts. It is in the second chapter of Genesis. The birds and animals were paraded before Adam "to see what he would call them." We are told that "Whatever the man called every living creature, that was its name." This story is revealing to us the power we have to name things and experiences. If we name them bad or disturbing, that is what they will be to us.

The birds represent ideas that come to us from the Lord or Spirit of God within us. How do you name your ideas? Many times we have named them "impractical," "impossible," "won't work," or some other negative classification. Let us now use this positive power of naming in a constructive way. When the Lord or God tells us to do something, let us accept it. If at first we do not see how it can work out, let us hold to the idea and know that at the right time and in the right way, the spirit of God will move through us to express and manifest that idea and nothing can prevent it.

Let us also use this naming power constructively regarding what seem to be negative people and situations. Remember the Biblical promise, "All things work together for good." The good is not the pain or hardship or challenge. The good is the patience, love, and understanding we develop in consciousness that enables us to rise above the negative challenge and this good brings peace of mind.

What shall it be? It is up to you. You have all you need within you to make positive and constructive decisions, for you have the light of truth, the Spirit of God, and He will always lead you aright.

THE PROTECTING PRESENCE

To some people it would seem that we need protection from the acts of God as well as the acts of man. The many climatic upheavals that have recently occurred are usually attributed to God since we do not know why they happen. According to this theory it would appear that God has gone mad, that He is really angry, killing thousands of people—men, women and children. There have been earthquakes, tornadoes, hurricanes, tidal waves, fires, volcanic eruptions, and avalanches; quite a few people have died.

I heard a religious leader seeking to console the bereaved with the statement that we must always be prepared, for we do not know when God is going to strike. The point he was making is that God caused the earthquake; it may not make sense to us for Him to kill such a large number of people in this manner, but we are not to question God's ways.

The truth is, God does not cause earthquakes or any other violent, eruptive changes in the earth. God does not kill people. God is the author of life and He wants us to live. If we were fully aware of our relationship with God and always followed the inner light there would be no misfortunes.

These climatic conditions and shifts in the earth's surface in the form of earthquakes are caused by the individual and collective consciousness of mankind. At the present time most people do not think or believe that their consciousness has anything to do with what happens in the world of events, but this is where they are mistaken. We are where we are, experiencing what we are because of our consciousness. Consciousness is made up of all our past thinking, feeling, believing, and of our experiences, both in this lifetime and in the many we have had before this one. The causes of some of our experiences in this life originated thousands of years ago. It makes no difference whether we believe this or not. We have always existed and we will always continue to exist.

There are some things that must be worked out in consciousness before we attain that state of consciousness that Jesus had, but we will all make it one day. We don't know and don't try to judge why people are involved in these climactic upheavals; in the same way we do not try to judge why good people get sick. Yet, we do not blame these things on God. God wants to help us rise above the negative states of consciousness and the experiences we bring upon ourselves. Getting angry at God only delays our receiving that help.

We know in our studies of truth that we are doing some things right, for we are not totally wrong. We have a degree of health, prosperity, happiness, and many other good things. However, we do not know all the truth about life and therefore we are also making some mistakes. Some of the mistakes are often disguised as righteous acts. There are also mistakes of not doing anything when we know we should. Now, the law of compensation does not cease to operate simply because I may be unaware of it or refuse to believe that there is such a principle. I can refuse to believe in the law of gravity but it will certainly work if I step off a tall building.

It is possible to protect ourselves from the possible negative consequences of our mistakes through what is termed the grace of God. Some people have had what seem to us miraculous help during some of these tragic happenings. No doubt it has been stated that they were saved by the grace of God. It is true, they were. But why didn't His grace save them all? His grace is all-powerful and can help us regardless of the severity of the incident we may be involved in. Receptivity to His grace, which is His love that seeks to help us, is developed through times of meditation. God can only do for us what He can do through our consciousness. We do not have to understand how all this happens, but we must believe and expect and be receptive to His help.

The Psalmist states, "He that dwelleth in the secret place of the Most High shall abide under the shadow of the Almighty." What he is saying is this: he who dwells in the consciousness of the presence of God, the one who knows and believes in the great power within him, will be protected and guided in ways that lead to health, happiness, and prosperity. The Secret Place is within you; it is the point of contact in consciousness with the great universal power we call God.

Consciousness determines experience. Jesus said, "To them that hath it shall be given and they shall have more abundance, but to them that hath not, even what they have shall be taken away." Human consciousness is developed through intellectual activity. Spiritual consciousness is developed through intuitive activity which takes place in meditation. We cannot think our way into the kingdom of God. We can't read enough books, attend enough seminars, or go to enough healing meetings expecting someone to give us the help we seek. All these things may be helpful in training and disciplining the intellect, but the development of spiritual consciousness, the consciousness that has real power to help, comes only through the regular practice of meditation, seeking the inner kingdom.

Spiritual consciousness can always protect us and help us rise above human consequences, even the ones set in motion through ignorance or foolishness or frustration. In fact if a person has practiced prayer he will be prevented from doing something negative when it seems that he cannot control the outer experience on the conscious, intellectual level.

This spiritual consciousness can also protect us from the acts of other people who would seek to do us harm. If thieves take something, the good will be replaced and we won't have to hate the thief. When we have the consciousness of God's protecting presence we do not have to curtail our normal, needed, or desired activities because of fear. Many people stay home, especially at night, simply because they are afraid that someone will harm them. They might even use the reasoning that we should not test God by going out when we know it might be dangerous to do so. When we have the consciousness, and know that we have it, it isn't a matter of testing God, it is a matter of trusting God. It is a matter of living by faith rather than living by fear. Testing God is doing something without the consciousness. It may be likened to a person who tries to lift a hundred pound weight without previous conditioning exercises.

The Psalmist also tells us that "Though a thousand shall fall at thy side and ten thousand at thy right hand, it shall not come nigh thee." Here again he is telling us that what happens to others does not have to happen to the one who abides in the consciousness of God's presence.

God's protecting help is available to everyone but we must have the consciousness through which He can work to help us. So keep on doing your spiritual exercises. Give even more time to the seeking of spiritual truth. Read the books, attend the seminars, classes, and services. In addition to these things be sure to take time to sit quietly in meditation each day. You don't need any special technique; you will develop your own. God speaking through one of the Biblical writers simply states it with, "Be still and know that I am God." Still all the intellectual activity that doubts and questions and know that God is all-powerful. He can solve any problem; He can heal any condition; He can prosper at any time. Know this, believe this and it will happen through you.

Regular, consistent effort is necessary in developing

spiritual consciousness. Spasmodic effort reaps spasmodic results. If you want the inner feeling of security, the realization and assurance that God is with you at all times, under all conditions, then meditate and pray when you feel like it and when you don't feel like it. As the inner spiritual consciousness is developed you will know it, you will feel it, and you will be blessed by it in many wonderful ways.

HOW TO DEAL WITH ANXIETY

Many thoughts pass through our minds each day; positive thoughts, negative thoughts, thoughts of good things to do and thoughts of unpleasant things to do. Some of these thoughts may originate in our own minds, but many of them are just a part of the mass thinking of humanity. Our minds are often like a radio; we tune in to the mass thinking of collective human consciousness. Some become fearful of these thoughts, thinking that these thoughts have power over them and will manifest in their lives. However, we should take heart in the realization of truth that of itself, thought has no power. It becomes powerful only when we serve it by accepting and believing it.

When someone makes a negative suggestion to us, that thought has no power over us unless we accept it as a possibility and give the power of our consciousness to it. For example when a person picks up the newspaper and reads something like an astrological forecast telling him the day will be bad for him, that thought has no power to make the day bad unless the individual accepts it and believes in it. And this is just what many people do to spoil their day.

For every experience in life there are two possible thoughts as to how to deal with that experience. Whatever way we choose becomes our master. The two possibilities are the human and the spiritual. Thought which is mostly dual in nature and based on appearances, tradition or human values is the human way. It is the way of experience and it is usually very difficult even if it produces a

101

little of what we might think of as good. The other way is the way of oneness, thought based on principle, on spiritual values.

Jesus said that we could not serve two masters. We cannot believe that we can be healed and at the same time believe that healing is impossible. One thought will be the master and we will serve it as a slave if it happens to be the negative one. When we try to serve both the positive and negative we are filled with anxiety, confusion, and discouragement.

Today there is much that a person can be concerned about, humanly speaking. Many are anxious about their need for supply. There is also a need for stability and peace in the world. Or it may be a need for healing. On the personal level there may be concern about the welfare of a relative, friend, or those less fortunate. Jesus gave us some good advice on how to deal with our anxious thought. He said, "Take no thought for your life."

You will note that this means that we should not take any "good" thought as well as "negative" thought. In other words we are not to try to think good into our experiences and we are not to try to think evil out of our lives. Some students think that the purpose of denials and affirmations is to make things happen in this way, but they are mistaken. Jesus' statement was very specific in suggesting that we give no thought to what we shall eat, drink, or wear. He used the analogy of the birds. They do not sow and harvest and store in barns. They are totally helpless and dependent on God to provide their food and God always does. When they have to eat there is an instinctive intelligence that leads them to food and water.

As for clothing Jesus said to consider the lilies of the field. They do not work, they do not spin, they do not think about how their needs will be fulfilled, and yet they are more beautifully clothed than the rich King Solomon. On the human level we spend a great deal of our time thinking about these human needs. Not only do we think much about what we shall eat but how we will get the money to buy the food. Much thought is given to dressing properly in order to be successful and to gain attention.

However, Jesus is saying to us that if we take no thought God will clothe us more beautifully than Solomon and provide food and all other needs. That is a fantastic promise and it is really true. Consider for a moment the food that you eat. You do not take thought about how it will be processed and used by the body; in fact, thought can interfere with the harmonious assimilation and use of that food. So "take no thought" is good advice.

"Take no thought for your life" means that we are not to take thought about what our children may or may not do; we are not to take thought about our work. It also means that we are not to set up personal goals and give a lot of thought to planning, plotting and trying to think things into existence through the use of visual imaging as some do in treasure mapping. Jesus even went so far as to say, "Take no thought for tomorrow," for we would have enough to deal with today. There is no need to be concerned with what tomorrow will bring. When the Hebrews escaped from Egypt with Moses, they were provided with manna for each day and they were not to take provisions for the next day.

In human thinking this advice of Jesus to take no thought seems like very poor advice and very impractical in this day and age. But it is very good and very practical when we understand what He is really talking about. To prove His point about the inadequacy of human, intellectual thought and planning He said, "Which of you, by taking thought, can add one cubit unto his stature?" The answer of course is no one. Many have tried to make things happen, even good things that should happen, but they have only experienced frustration and more anxiety. That's what anxiety is—the thought and feeling that we will not get what we need or desire.

If we are not to take thought and try to figure out how

our good will come or how something unpleasant can be dealt with, what are we to do? Jesus' advice is this: "Seek ye first the kingdom of God and his righteousness and all these things will be added unto you." To seek the kingdom doesn't mean we won't do anything. In fact when we truly seek the kingdom we will do more things but in a different way. Seeking the kingdom doesn't mean we won't think anymore, but we will think in a different way. Instead of our trying to think God into a course of action we will let Him think through us. Jesus expressed this as, "Not my will, but thine be done." Instead of intellectually and personally dreaming up solutions, we let God reveal to us, intuitively, the right solutions. Intuition is God thinking through us, guiding, directing, healing, and prospering us.

Instead of getting into a stew of negative thought we turn within to the true Source, God, and let go. We become still in the silence of the inner kingdom and listen for the still small voice. We don't try to figure anything out. We don't try to make determinations. We become still and listen for divine answers. Answers and solutions come when we let go of the toil of human thought. Jesus also stated, "Of mine own self I can do nothing but the Father within me can do all things." Jesus did a lot of things, but they were done by God through Him. When we become still in thought and let God think through us, He can do much more for us. We will do and accomplish much more than we have before and we will do it more easily. We will discover greater joy and happiness in what we are led to do.

Becoming still raises consciousness and makes it more powerful to produce good. Where there is harmony in consciousness there is peace and fulfillment. When we are in tune with the spiritual laws of life things are added easily. Supply comes forth without struggle or deviousness or selfishness. We do not have to hate, fight, be resistant or seek revenge. We enter into a consciousness of trust, knowing that God will provide all we need.

When we seek to help someone we should remember to take no thought. Do not dwell on problems or even treat them. Instead of mentally trying to eliminate the sickness by trying to think it out of existence we seek to raise our consciousness to a higher level of knowing that God is the guiding light, the healing life, the all-sufficient substance to provide for all the needs of everyone. Jesus said, "If I be lifted up I will draw all men unto me." This lifting up is in consciousness. To know and let the truth express in consciousness is to be an instrument for true healing. When the individual needing healing tunes in to this consciousness he will receive his help. These healings may be slower in manifesting but they will be permanent. Mental results produced by "taking thought" do not last. The quick and easy way often turns out to be the short-lived and hard way. The inner way of intuitive thought, the way of the inner kingdom, the raising of consciousness to a higher realization that God is the answer, that He will and can provide—this is the true answer.

THE BIRTH OF CHRIST IN YOU

Many of the well-known statements about Jesus that are especially associated with Christmas actually come from our Old Testament. For example, Matthew quotes the great prophet Isaiah as saying, "Behold, a virgin shall conceive, and bear a son, and shall call his name Immanuel." (Isaiah 7:14)

This particular passage has such theological overtones that its mystical significance has been lost. The statement was made by the prophet to King Ahaz over 700 years before the time of Jesus. It was a time of great crisis in Hebrew history. It was given to the king for reassurance at this time that the Lord would protect him and the nation but we have come to think of it as a prophecy about the coming birth of Jesus.

To the Hebrew people the king, when anointed, was their Messiah. Their expectation for the coming of a Messiah was therefore a king who would be of the caliber of David their great king. Jesus never claimed to be a king. He said His kingdom was not of this world. He had no intention of setting up an earthly kingdom and ruling over people.

The occasion for this statement made by the prophet Isaiah was this: the kingdom of Israel, which had been founded by Saul and expanded and prospered by David and Solomon, was divided upon the death of Solomon into two kingdoms—Israel to the north, and Judah to the south. The big threat to many of the smaller kingdoms at that time was Assyria. To meet this threat the smaller kingdoms wanted to form a military alliance to face and, it was hoped, to defeat the Assyrians. Israel began by forming an alliance with Syria, a small kingdom to her north. These two wanted Judah to join this alliance, but King Ahaz wasn't sure that even with her help the three of them could defeat Assyria. Israel and Syria were actually planning to attack Judah if she did not join the alliance and under this pressure the prophet Isaiah told the king to stand firm and not join the alliance. The prophet also told the king not to appeal to Assyria for help to meet this threat but to trust in the Lord.

One day the king and the prophet were out surveying the water supply for the city. The prophet continued to assure the king that trust in the Lord would save the nation. For further assurance he told the king to ask for a sign, any sign he wanted, to prove that the words of the prophet would be true. King Ahaz said he would not ask for a sign: "I will not ask; neither will I tempt the Lord." The prophet said he would give him a sign anyway. He said to the king, "Do you see that young woman down at the watering hole drawing water? She is expecting a child. Before that child is old enough to think and make decisions about good and evil the alliance between Israel and Syria will be broken." He said the child's name would be called Immanuel, which means "God is with us."

The king did not listen to the prophet so that the sign had no meaning for him. He appealed to Assyria for help. The Assyrians came down and soundly defeated Syria and Israel and for this Judah had to pay dearly, not only with money but with the loss of her freedom as well.

If Ahaz had listened to Isaiah and had done what he suggested it would have changed the course of Hebrew history. That prophetic utterance was true for Ahaz; it was true for Jesus. It is true for you and me today, and it will be true for the many generations to come who will need the help it offers, for it is a mystical statement. The child of prophecy named Immanuel is not a physical child. The child represents the birth of Christ in our consciousness, the recognition in us of our spiritual identity. The birth of the child, whether we think of this child as one being born at the time of Isaiah the prophet or whether we think of it as the birth of Jesus, is the moment of inner realization that God is with us, that He has always been with us and that He will always be with us. Many people today think of God as being up in the sky. They are looking forward to a time when God will make an appearance on the earth in human form. The birth has not taken place and they therefore appeal to Assyria, mystically speaking, instead of trusting in the Lord to help them in their time of crisis. But there are some who have caught a glimpse of the great truth of being.

Isaiah refers to these people in this way, "The people that walked in darkness have seen a great light." (Isaiah 9:2) The great light is the truth that you and I and everyone are all children of God. We are spiritual beings with infinite possibilities of good within us. Many are walking in darkness today and are actually blind to this truth even though they think they are filled with light. Who are they? They are those who think of themselves as sinners or simply as human beings with many limitations and subject to all the physical laws that seem to hold them in bondage to sickness, poverty, and other forms of limitation. In their blindness they affirm that they believe and trust in the Lord, but they do not know who the Lord is. They keep hoping and expecting a Lord to come to them as a historical character. Isaiah is suggesting, as did Jesus, that we rely upon the Lord who is within us. Even if the divine realization, the virgin birth, the intuitive perception is only a child, we should rely upon it, for only this inner Lord can save us from any crisis.

Isaiah stated further, "For unto us a child is born, unto us a son is given; and the government shall be upon his shoulder." When we rely upon our human powers of thought we find that the governing of our lives is a burden that causes us much grief, anguish, sorrow, and frustration. But there is One within you and me that has the answer that will help us meet any crisis successfully. The plan of salvation is up to Him.

"His name shall be called Wonderful, Counsellor, the mighty God, the Everlasting Father, the Prince of Peace." (Isaiah 9:6) He will counsel you; He will instruct and teach you in the way you should go. His guidance and assurance will lead to peace; there will be no end to his rule of peace within you and in your life. "He shall be for a sanctuary." (Isaiah 8:14) No matter what you may be going through right now, you can abide in Him and find peace, happiness, and joy. When we discover this inner Father or Prince of Peace we are amazed that He can do so much through us and for us.

You may have thought the world would have to change before your problem or problems could be solved. But when you see the great light and trust in Him, the inner light, you discover that you can have peace now; nothing has to change outside of you, only inside of you. You do not have to wait until someone changes his or her opinion about you. You do not have to have recognition or acceptance from anyone. You do not have to wait until the economy is straightened out before you can be prospered, for you will have the assurance that the Lord of your being will provide for all your needs. You will also discover that as you make the inner changes in consciousness, outer changes will be made, but they will be made easily and effortlessly by God working through you. God will use us instead of us using God.

Jesus said, "My yoke is easy and my burden is light." This was true for Him because He always let God work through Him and because of this Jesus was always the master of every situation.

Christmas reminds us of the great truth of the divine

realization that is possible for us, the birth of Christ in consciousness. This is truly a virgin birth, for there is no need of Joseph, the intellect. You cannot think yourself into the kingdom or discover through the mind the full awareness of who and what you are as a spiritual being. You do not have to wonder as Mary did, "How can this be?" Many times we do wonder how something so great can happen to us. But all we need to do is to be still and know, believe and trust, and let it happen. The realization cannot be forced and even though many "storm the kingdom," as Jesus said, they cannot enter it.

If we are patient with ourselves, the birth will take place, but we must be persistent in our inner search. Don't be disappointed if after you experience the divine awakening your outer world isn't transformed miraculously overnight. Jesus' birth didn't radically change anything outwardly at first, but eventually the change was brought about. Every time you become still in quiet, non-intellectual meditation you are growing. The growth may seem slow, but forget about all the human wants and desires that seek instant gratification. One day you will realize that what seemed slow wasn't slow after all: it was a firm and lasting growth.

Isaiah said to the people, "Associate yourselves, O ye people, and ye shall be broken in pieces." (Isaiah 10:9) If we join the alliance, which mystically means if we try to rely upon outer religious forms to save us, if we depend upon others for happiness, or if we place our faith and trust in something outside of ourselves, we shall be disappointed. It is faith in your inner Lord that will save you and lift you up. He will show you what you should do outwardly, and He will guide you to those with whom you should associate and work. He will tell you what to do outwardly regarding your supply and your health. The Lord within you will redeem you; your joy in Him will be Wonderful and your Peace will be without end.

YOU CAN MAKE IT

When Samuel was a young boy his mother, Hannah, took him to the temple at Shiloh where Eli the priest could train him to become a priest in the temple. One night after he arrived there he was asleep and heard someone call him. Samuel thought it was the old priest Eli calling him so he went to Eli and said, "Here am I." Eli said, "I called not, lie down again." Samuel went back to his room and went to sleep again. After a while he heard his name called again. He thought sure this must be Eli so he went again and said, "Here am I." But the old priest had not called Samuel and he told Samuel to go back to sleep. So, again, Samuel went to sleep and again heard his name called and again went back to Eli. This time Eli realized what was happening so he told Samuel to go back and lie down and if he heard his name called again he was to remain there and simply say, "Speak, Lord, for thy servant heareth."

Samuel did as he was instructed by Eli and sure enough the Lord did call Samuel. Samuel did as he was instructed and said, "Speak, for thy servant heareth." As Samuel listened he heard the Lord say to him, "Behold, I will do a thing in Israel, at which both the ears of every one that heareth it shall tingle." (I Sam. 3:11)

The Lord was trying to get Samuel's attention. Samuel thought he was being called by someone outside of himself, the old priest Eli, for the Scripture says, "Now Samuel did not yet know the Lord, neither was the word of the Lord yet revealed unto him ." (I Sam. 3:7) We are like Samuel in that the Lord is trying to get our attention and we are so focused on outer living that we do not hear

111

Him. The difficulty arises because in many instances we think we have to get the Lord's attention. We think God is so preoccupied with the needs of the world and all the people in it that He doesn't even know we exist. But this is not true.

In describing the time of Samuel the Scriptures tell us, "The word of the Lord was precious in those days; there was no open vision." There were many people going to the place of worship offering sacrifices and praying and yet they did not know the Lord. There were not many people then who had the awareness that the Lord was the presence of God within them.

The word of the Lord is still precious today. In comparison with the total population of this world, there are not very many people who know the Lord. Of those who pray to a lord outside of them, many think this lord is in heaven which they believe to be up in the sky. They are not aware of the Lord of their being, the Lord within them. This is true for many who are seeking truth even in the metaphysical movements. The reason for this is that in many instances individuals are trying to get the Lord to do their bidding. When they go apart to pray they are often loaded with many requests and petitions. They may even have lists of things that they want the Lord God to do for them. They think that the obtaining of these things will make them happy and successful. They may even spend a great deal of their prayer time visualizing these things as being theirs already, thinking, sincerely, that this is helping God to bring them into their lives.

When we really become aware of the inner Lord we find that this type of effort is not necessary. We do not have to outline our lives for God. We do not have to tell Him what needs to be healed. We do not have to tell Him how to make things right. We realize that much of this mental effort is a hindrance to getting the right answers from the Lord. What is necessary is for us to learn to listen. We need to learn to be still and say as did Samuel, "Speak, Lord, for thy servant heareth." When our desire is to know the Lord's will or plan, He will give us a vision for our lives that is far superior to anything we could dream up on the personal level. In fact, when what we *want* to do in life is in agreement with what we *should* do, we have a true guarantee for success.

Your Lord knows you better than you know yourself. When you release all personal plans and are completely willing to accept and do what He tells you, you will find that He will inspire you with a vision for your life which when accepted will fill your heart with joy. His plan may seem, in the beginning, to be more challenging than your personal plan. But remember, with God's help you can always make it. When you know that God is with you, you will have an inner confidence and assurance that you can do whatever He guides you to do. You cannot fail with God.

When you make the determination that you will follow His guidance you may find that in the beginning you will be told to do things that may seem tedious, boring, and uninteresting. You may have to give up a few things also. It may be a habit or a relationship and you may think this to be a big sacrifice. But this is only a necessary preparation for the great things that lie in store for you.

God's whole, wonderful, and great plan is not often revealed in one vision. It would be too overwhelming for the human mind to accept. This is true not only for the challenges but also for the great possibilities. The human mind is often very skeptical and pessimistic. It is also reluctant to let go of the "bird in the hand." It would rather hold on to something that it already has rather than accept the plan of the Lord. However, if you want to make progress it is imperative that you settle down and be willing to accept the Lord's guidance. There is no other way to find happiness in life. Many people put this off. They continue to struggle trying to demonstrate their own personal plans. They work hard at this and they are sincere in many instances. But they will not achieve happiness or success in this way.

If we are to become intimately acquainted with the Lord we must seek Him. To do this we must study and meditate and this must be done daily, not weekly or annually. We must be willing to set up a daily regimen of study of spiritual truth at home and in class work. We must devote more time to reading good truth books. We must give up the desire for overnight or weekend spiritual growth which we think will solve our problems once and for all. Spiritual growth usually takes place slowly. The ambitious human intellect may protest, saying that Jesus said that we could ask whatsoever we wanted and it would be done. When we put this promise back into a proper perspective we find that He said this would be true if we asked "in His name," that is, if we abide in Him and His words abide in us, then we could ask. In that state of consciousness we would never ask for some of the things we have been asking for. We wouldn't ask for something that would not be for our good or for the good of someone else.

It is a tremendous relief when we put our lives in the hands of the Lord. We can do that by affirming and realizing, "Not my will, but thy will be done." That prayer should be on our lips daily and in our hearts at all times. We must be patient and wait until we feel His presence urging us on. As we turn to Him daily He will guide us in a way that will bring inner peace and outer peace. He will make His presence known in a way that will be clear to us. He will lead us in a way that we would never have known. When this happens, the study of truth, and the living of truth, will become a pleasure and a joy.